BUFFALO JUMP

June 1, 1999
Winnipeg

To Barbara,
with thanks for
coming to the
reading.

Rita Moir

BUFFALO JUMP

A WOMAN'S TRAVELS

RITA MOIR

COTEAU BOOKS

Edited by Robert Currie.

Cover Image by Noblet Design Group.
Cover and book design by Duncan Campbell.
Printed and bound in Canada.
Author photo by Donna Ratcliffe.

The author wishes to acknowledge support from the Cultural Services Branch of the BC Ministry of Small Business, Tourism, and Culture.

The publisher gratefully acknowledges the financial assistance of the Saskatchewan Arts Board, the Canada Council for the Arts, the Government of Canada through the Book Publishing Industry Development Program (BPIDP), and the City of Regina Arts Commission, for its publishing program.

Canadian Cataloguing in Publication Data

Moir, Rita, 1952–
Buffalo jump, a woman's travels
ISBN 1-55050-144-5

1. Moir, Rita, 1952–   —Journeys—Alberta.
2. Alberta—Description and travel.
3. Canada—Description and travel
4. Head-Smashed-In Buffalo Jump Provincial Historic Site (Alta.)
I. Title.

FC3667.3.M657 1999   917.123'4   C99-920028-3
F1076.M657 1999

COTEAU BOOKS	AVAILABLE IN THE US FROM
401-2206 Dewdney Ave.	General Distribution Services
Regina, Saskatchewan	85 River Rock Drive, Suite 202
Canada S4R 1H3	Buffalo, New York, USA 14207

Dedicated to my Mother and my Nana
To my father who gave me
my love of the prairies
To my mother who gave me
her stories

BUFFALO JUMP

THE ROAD OUT

Today my odometre will turn to 270,000 kilometres I will drive a thousand more. I will sweep through the mountain corridors from BC into Alberta, past the metal windmills on their hillside at Cowley.

I'm happier than when I shut myself away in January and only told a few people what had happened. Mostly I'm okay now. Hey Connor, I say to my dog, You've outlasted them all.

I'm talking to him in the rearview mirror, and behind him the mountains recede as we open into the prairies. I haven't been to the prairies yet with this emotion. The Crowsnest Pass and the Buffalo Jump, the Head-Smashed-In Buffalo Jump, have become my hinge place, where the closed door of dark mountains opens into prairie and light, where all that's kept in is let out.

I once lived on prairie like this. So did my mother.

And my Nana. But we've never talked about it much.

Yesterday I finished cleaning the house before leaving. On a flat brown bag in the piles of paper on the staircase, the reminder, "Make chutney," then scribbled down in the corner, "My mother is the narrative link." "Make chutney" has a neat tick mark by it. Job done. Twenty-one jars.

Connor shifts around in the back seat. He's 12 now, stiff in the joints but still game for the car ride. He's a big black long-haired setter or retriever, it's always been a guess which. Connor's the kind of dog who's friendly with most everyone, but he's mine and I'm his.

The windmills greet me like a line of friendly visitors from outer space, a big line of them on the crest of the hill, their arms twirling arhythmically, as if they're waving. The wind picks up, and they are Olympians, skaters slightly out-of-sync in their side by side wind-driven sit-spins, their act of joy welcoming me to the prairies.

I pull in out of the rain with all the other cars at the Pincher Creek Husky, and the soup of the day is Cream of Potato and Bacon, spuds and pork. It's good, thick, rainy day road food that sticks to my ribs.

I veer north of the #3 highway onto the secondary dirt road to Head-Smashed-In Buffalo Jump. On my way there, I'll see other windmills I've visited before. They stand like slender egg-beaters, silver ribbons of metal against the sky. The fallen windmill I visit each year is still there, like a crumpled dinosaur, a wounded mammoth lying on the prairie.

There are no directional signs on this backroad. I rarely use my own reckoning, because I hate getting lost, but today I seem able to feel my way through the prairie.

I drive through miles and miles of open rolling backroad, glad there is hardly anyone on the road today, and I'm happy to see so few cars in the parking lot at the Head-Smashed-In Buffalo Jump Interpretive Centre. The day is cool and Connor can stay in the car.

Out on the buffalo jump, out past the interpretive centre, above the ledge where the buffalo plunged to their death, I am alone. I hear only the wind, and see far east into the coulees, turn around and around to the mountains and prairie. The cliff the buffalo plunged over is layers of rock, tinged rust red in some places, with lichen and moss in others. As I look out and over the prairie, I don't think of smashed or dying bodies. Instead, below the jump I see the thickets of wolfberry and chokecherry as thick and high as alder. The buffalo themselves have been dead so many years they have fertilized and changed into this lushness in the lee of the cliffside.

I simply feel movement and wind, this wind I was raised in, always from the west. Twenty years ago I lived here in southern Alberta. When the wind blew from the east and the trees bent the wrong way, it was like watching a movie going backward. Here at the buffalo jump, with the wind blowing from the west, as it should, I can see and hear so far and breathe so deeply that I am smiling.

In January, when I hid myself away, I read how the trails of the buffalo through bush or prairie led people to water, to the trees and shade and the game, to rivers they had to cross. I read how mother buffalo would ferry the young ones on their shoulders across deep streams. I read how miles and miles of buffalo would hold up trains for days. I read how buffalo wallows, where they rolled deep and long, would provide shelter for settlers, or places for water to pool.

Standing at the buffalo jump, I wonder what fields they roamed, what places they moved to? Where should I move to? How do I keep on going? How did they lead the way?

After twenty years living in the mountains of British Columbia, I'm still not certain why I'm there. In some way I still resist it. It is a common enough feeling for any prairie person living there, our attitudes a bore to British Columbians, I am certain. My Nana once visited BC and said she only wanted to take an auger and drill a hole through a mountain to let some sun through. I can't find silence in my view of the mountains. It's crowded, like a non-stop talker. I want to back away from the mountains, like from a person crowding me at a party. They make me go inside myself to escape. I can only comprehend that the mountains are my forge, my compressor, and I am glad today to be free of them. On the prairies I can go outside myself. I can breathe again.

Right now I want no people, no sympathy, no talking. I want nothing but quiet and miles and miles of solid colours in big expanses.

Back on the road, the photos I take are fields of canola and flax, a horizon of yellow and blue under a blue sky. There are tall golden grasses, cat tails with mountains and sky behind. Skimming through snow and sun from one world to the next, mountain to prairie, on this day, on this most beautiful road in this country, it's as if only here the ground could speak directly to the sky.

In Medicine Hat, at another Husky, an old couple sits at the table next to me, and after we exchange the ritual road greetings of where we came from and where we're going, they order the Cream of Mushroom soup. She nudges him and they bow their heads in prayer. As I rise to leave, the woman tells me the Lord will watch over and bless me. And she tells me to drive safely.

I pull safely across the road into the Ranchmen Motel, smiling at this first casual encounter, this small blessing bestowed upon my trip. I start unloading for the night. Connor out first, then dog food, water bowl, his sleeping bag, radio, my own stuff. I travel heavy when I can. All the emergency gear in the back, flashlights, candles, tools, my yellow rain gear still smelling faintly of bleach and streaked with blood from gutting fish on the days I went out fishing on my last trip to Nova Scotia.

I unload a small cooler of scallops. They are all I have left from my fisherman. Last year when we were still together I carried these same scallops all the way from Nova Scotia to BC Now I'm packing them from BC back across the prairies, in a little pink styrofoam cooler my Nova Scotia brother made for me. Connor and I have travelled back and forth between BC and Nova Scotia over and over these last years. It was getting confusing, this traipsing back and forth. But that ended in January. I can see now that the scallops are really the last thing I have of my fisherman to hold onto. Here I am, like a child with a wounded bird or a blanket, dragging the scallops along with me as I return to my family on the prairie. Each night the scallops go into a motel's freezer, and are returned to me at five the next morning when I head back on the road.

Each morning as I set out, I hit a small bird. The collision is shocking, but in their hundreds the birds light and dart up off the highway, as if playing chicken, as if, like me, they are too anxious for the morning, and there is nothing we would do to alter this.

On CBC, four fiddlers play from across the country. Some saw the strings, some fly to the skies. Their styles and rhythms take me to all the places I've lived or worked or visited, from Nova Scotia to Alberta, from Ontario to

Newfoundland. There is Maritime Celtic, prairie slow dance, and I can almost hear the floorboards of an old hall creaking to the dancers. I notice how much faster and lighter the Easterners play, but where is a Metis fiddler from Manitoba?

My mind crowds and empties – all set off by the fiddle music – travelling in Cape Breton with my fisherman friend, fishboats on the Atlantic, my Manitoba high school play about Louis Riel and the founding of Manitoba, about the Metis, and about Riel's last speech. All this jumbles and tumbles and breathes with the music and the prairie wind.

Late that second morning I'm near Weyburn. I don't know anything about Weyburn, except it's some kind of prairie mythical name. Hockey, W.O. Mitchell, and Tommy Douglas (but we all like to claim him). At home I keep a painting I copied from a bottle of Saskatchewan rye whisky, made in Weyburn. The painting comes off the front of a Hallowe'en costume I made – fashioning myself as a bottle of Saskatchewan rye – a stapled together cardboard costume I could barely move in, and on the front I'd painted the label, just like the one on the real bottle from back in the 1970s, grain elevators, nodding golden rye, and the sky and land orange and yellow, gold and brown.

The Weyburn Red Wings, I think as I wait for the train to go by before I can cross the tracks into town. I am falling into the stupor, the rhythm of the wheels on the track, a rhythm that rocks me forward and back, to tracks

I crossed in all my prairie downtowns and ravines – so many of us recent immigrants or a few generations from somewhere. When my family lived in Manitoba the Brandon Wheat Kings played against the Weyburn Red Wings, and the names of our guys, Juha Widing and Bruce Bonk, poured like honey or clattered like ice cubes off our prairie tongues.

Yah, we could say Juha Widing (such a mellifluous name to untrained tongues, You-ha Veeding) or lefsa, say it or eat it, we could say holopchis and if we couldn't we'd call them jalopies, eat yule kake, not like yule cake, but you-la caw-caw, or bannock or dark rye from North Winnipeg. We savoured tandoori or venison, pheasant and shortbread, paella and gold-eye, egg rolls, Mulligan stew, curries and strawberry shortcake. We knew lots of names, lots of nations, lots of kinds of food. We were prairie people and we opened our oven doors and sometimes our hearts to each other. My mother did anyway, no matter how many friends we brought home for supper.

I'm making myself hungry just thinking of it, sitting here daydreaming as the train rolls on and on.

I pull up to an RCMP car parked by a fast food take-out, gambling they will be hospitable enough to ignore the rust patches like potato scabs on my car. There's a twitch of a smile as they look at me and my old dog and my old car, then direct me to downtown where I can walk and find a restaurant away from the highway.

I park the car in the shade, give Connor some water and a walk, and leave him there with the windows rolled down. I look into several restaurants but I am restless, seeking something I can't find. Some smell, some kind of booth, some kind of smile. Finally a clerk in a drugstore says, You want The Captain's Table. The Captain's Table, in the middle of the prairie. The irony, the emotional jab, is either going to be just right, a survivable poke at the sore, or a mistake, I decide, and take the risk. I walk to the strip mall, the kind where you can drive on blacktop right up to the front door.

I sit at the back where I can listen to the waitresses. The smell is seafood and chips, the talk is prairie – tornadoes and crops. I relax into the leather padding of all the restaurants I've ever worked in, and listen to the kitchen talk, as reassured as a child listening to the murmur of her parents' voices in the night. I took the scallops out to thaw for you, says one waitress to another, and I smile as I add my silent lines to their conversation. Would you like to see the scallops I have in the car? I don't mean bragging like, You wanna see scallops, take a look at these!

I want to say, Wait, I have something to show you. Aren't these amazing, these Bay of Fundy scallops I've carried so far? The meat in them is as big as a baby's fist. It was here, on the map, here on the Bay of Fundy. Oh, the boats I got to go on, the man who opened that life to me for a while. I could tell them of my first trip on his scallop dragger, of 15 hours on the rolling ocean, how proud I was not to get sick, how I'd read somewhere that when you feel seasick, seek the horizon, a straight line to restore your balance, about the voices on the scanner, terse or bored or gossiping, how fast the men worked the heavy chains of the drags, how quickly their hands flew, shucking the scallops.

Or the day when the whale slid below the boat, and Look, I said, my eyes straining deep into the water, There are two whales. He moved over next to me, his ocean eyes so much sharper through dark water, and he said, Those are only its fins – look deeper – and I did, the long slow body coming and coming beneath us forever, my breath held, that such magnificence could go on forever, could play with us so gently.

But I don't say any of this. I just finish my cod and chips and get up and pay my bill so I can get back on the road fast before I think any more about him.

When you lose equilibrium, seek the horizon.

The miles and the music and my dog, so solid in the back seat, lift me again. Near Estevan, I get out of the car, and lie on the roadside to take wide pictures of the sky, close-ups of silver foxtail in the breeze, purple grasses, hills as voluptuous as hips, and a buffalo stands before them, watching me.

It stands solid, large, calm, the hump of its back fitting into the hips of the hills.

There is only one tape with me that expresses the

freedom I feel. Hey, I write to a friend back in BC, on the postcard of high clouds in a blue Saskatchewan sky, how many times can you play Ode to Joy?

In the prairie night I hear coyotes. There are so many coyotes so close by that my dog and I sit up to listen. We aren't afraid because we've heard coyotes for years. They surround my log house in the bush back in BC where I've lived half my life, and my dog all his long life. They yip and play and throw their voices. I turn off the radio and listen. Whenever we travel, they seem to greet us the first two days as we come into the prairie. They make strange, happy, minor then major harmonies, and I can almost believe they're singing to us.

I am happy to hear the coyotes' voices, as if they are calling me to join their singing. It's the important voices, the human kind, back in BC I can't listen to anymore. I've had to walk away from my role as a reporter, holding microphones to the faces of important men and helping them tell their stories. I'm tired of trying to look powerful, with short hair and shoulder pads, as if they would respect me more. Besides, after a while the stories are all the same, just repeated year after year.

Later on I look at a picture of my niece, then an old one of myself. A swinging ponytail, mud puddles, dogs and gardens, making my own adventures along silted banks of the Red River. I stop cutting my hair, start pulling it back in a ponytail as if I belonged in a tree fort or a barn.

There is something appealing about being a girl again and not giving a damn for anyone else's opinion.

I dream I am in some trouble in Vancouver. In the dream, I am frantic, out of place, can't get home, can't escape the trouble. I run out of the basement suite into the fenced yard. I hear voices coming to me. My mother strides up the street toward me, a niece on either side. My mother takes my hand and says, Let's get you out of here.

The plan for this trip is to visit my parents and family who live in Minnesota. And then I will drive with my mother to her family reunion in Ontario. We'll continue east to the Atlantic to see my brother in Nova Scotia, and travel around Cape Breton. I may see my fisherman. We've talked on the phone some, long distance. It's all right. I'll be all right. Sometimes I even say goodbye smiling.

Then Mum and I will head back to Minnesota for Mum and Dad's 50th wedding anniversary. I'll travel alone again after that, see my brother in Winnipeg, and maybe go check out where Mum was born in southern Manitoba.

I'm curious about the reunion in Ontario, since I've never been to such a large family gathering, but I feel no tie to that place or the family that remains and really all I want to do is be with my mother. She's 75. I am 42. We have 8,000 miles of highways and backroads ahead of us. I realize I think ahead in miles, behind in kilometres – clicks on the odometre – and the backroads I don't try to calibrate.

For two years now I've been having dog dreams. In each dream three young black dogs, rangy and wobbling and strong, romp toward me down the backroad, to greet me and my old black dog.

In another, the young dream-dog heeling to my left moves over to allow Connor his rightful place and slows his pace to match Connor's stiffer, lumbering gait.

I always know the message – it's just the emotion I can't handle.

But the buffalo dreams confuse me.

In one, I have had to slaughter a pregnant buffalo. I think she was badly injured, but later I question whether this was so.

I have even stripped her hide, then kneeling beside her, I push and push, forcing a kind of death labour, her sides heave, and she delivers three small buffalo, each could be held in your hand, each wrapped in a quilt of buffalo hide. They emerge with other gifts from her body, jerky, hides, meat, small cradles. The small buffalo, as small as kittens, are not breathing. My sister Donna is with me, and I teach her how to do CPR, small heart massages, as I once did on a baby chick hung up in the fence, and they begin to squirm.

I kneel on the prairie by the mother buffalo, covered in blood and wind, and wonder why I didn't try harder to help her live. She looks like meat on a hook, like bears I have butchered. The small buffalo curl up in fresh wood shavings, and my cat Dylan begins nursing them.

The only connection this dream has to anything I know is the act of butchering a large animal, and to wind, piercing and keening. Butchering and wind I know intimately.

On the road alone southeast of Weyburn I listen to composer Scott Macmillan's Celtic Mass for the Sea. Like the scallops, the Mass has become my transition from Nova Scotia. There are layers and layers and layers, taking me deeper, with warm pockets, like a swimmer, or a listener. It is religious and of faith, elemental, and sometimes, when it threatens to become too sombre, erupts into wild fiddle music. As the chorus sings of great whales and giant waves, I surge up and over hills of prairie, dip down again, huge rolls of hay, the gold of wheat, heaving in and out of view.

I am feeling my way. Nothing is deliberate or clear in this process of separation and rebuilding, although I begin to have some glimmer that I need to regain faith, that I am trying to build a structure that can take me through loss. A structure that will hook my bones together, that can help me lift in the wind. Something that will help me past the days when I've tripped on the woodshed steps and smashed my fingers between ice and logs, and howled alone in circles around and around my living room, holding my smashed fingers high to the ceiling, moaning in self-pity and loneliness and laughing at the pathetic spectacle I make even to myself. Even my old deaf dog tires of listening to me.

In those days, I sometimes feel I have my arms wrapped around my own waist, to keep my ribs and heart from falling out. In January, I take down all my Margaret Laurence from the bookshelves, reread her as if she is my catechism. I reason that if I can hold tight and make it through January, I will have proven myself. In the depths of that month, when I read about the buffalo, I learn their backbones and ribs were made into toboggans. I imagine myself a toboggan, I imagine myself the strength of a buffalo. I am Hagar in a seaside shack, Morag on a train, finding what our spines are made of, whether we can carry burdens, and like a toboggan, whip screaming laughing down a snowy hillside.

As the prairie rolls on and on, I understand how much I want my mother in my geography, on these prairie hillsides and ravines. The curious phrase, "My mother is the narrative link," repeats in my head, and I begin to understand why I've written it on scrap after scrap of paper as it came to me, was forgotten, found again in some pile of paper as I cleaned, or scribbled on an envelope, each time the phrase forgotten and reinvented. It won't leave me alone. As I drive further and further, I realize I want my mother to be the narrative link that makes my place in all of this real. It dawns on me that I want to have the right to belong.

On this long rolling journey that we will make together, she will tell me the stories of babies dying and unmarked graves, of long train trips, of women leaving husbands, of unlikely saviours in prairie blizzards. She will stretch her hands back across history for me, bringing back dead ones, ones who for her have never died, and with her stories in her one hand, she will link her other hand with mine, and give them to me so I can bring them forward in my turn.

I realize she can release me from the everyday, the grocery lists and dead batteries, smashed fingers and loneliness, the scrabbling over details like chickens at bark beetles; she can help me to be bigger. And though I'll only begin to understand this much later, her stories will settle into my geography, give calcium to my bones.

I understand that I want her images and my own – big images, this claim to history. I want big vistas, strong animals, ragged prairie rocks, large graveyards full of stories and tragedy. I don't want bickering, muttered sarcasms, crippling. I don't want increments. I want vastness, sweat, art transforming, gravestones chipped by moss and lichen, mountains and big skies in the Crowsnest, buffalo poised to jump with the thundering herd behind them, large skies and broken bones before them. I want truths too large to live, exaggeration sweeping away timidity, little bits, and maybes, I want the little pieces to add to large ones, nothing wasted. I want wheels pulverizing prairie roads, the road wearing down my bones. I don't want videos of wind, I want wind. I want screaming rain in the prairies, and greasy strange hotel keepers, and the safe haven of the Maynard Motel on Main Street in Moose Jaw. I want stories and stories and stories of who we are. I don't want cushions and airline movies, not mostly. Only when I can't care any more. I sicken and cringe from this life of voice mail and e-mail and internets and death stars and political meetings around long tables in grim basements. Where are the old people, the old books, the babies, and the wind? Where are the stories and songs? I become driven and tired like a crazed pioneer, battling through horrid wind and frozen lashes and screaming at the exhausted dog beside me, looking for the neighbour with stories, real stories, and a warm fire.

On this trip, my mother will tell me stories of her life on the prairie, and later, I will cross and recross the prairie alone. The voices in her stories will begin to people the small shacks, to ride on the trains. They will talk to me, yet not take me over, because those places are my own, too, with stories and songs they haven't heard. It's odd, I suppose, but it was at the Buffalo Jump, alone in the wind, that her stories began singing for me. Odd, because the Buffalo Jump is not my own, as the ocean was not my own. When I stood at the jump, I understood that in that particular place of history, I'm a visitor; there are thousands of years of stories above and below those cliffs. Yet the silence there, the vastness, hit me, hollowed me inside out and back again, like the ocean, like the first thunderous chords from a church organ.

After many trips there and back and forth across the prairie, looking so far out on the coulees, I began to see and hear my own prairie stories, the voices of my own women crazed or tired enough that they once heard voices on the wind, and now I am hearing theirs.

I want to say: Their stories aren't big ones. They aren't shipwrecks. They aren't wars. But standing at the Buffalo Jump, I realized that their stories are as big as the place itself, and that only there could I be big enough to hear them, see long enough back across the prairie, be quiet enough to listen to their silences.

I know the buffalo jump was a place of huge pain, of herds going over, of death and bloodshed. But in the quiet there, I also know a buffalo jump is a place of stories, of imagination, where a leap is a transition. The buffalo jump gave me enough distance, back to the mountains, out to the prairies, to take a longer view, to make my own transitions, to listen to what isn't being said. Prairie stories sometimes told with silences.

The buffalo jump, the silence and the distance there, helped me to understand that I can have my own places, my own stories, my own songs to the prairie. Stories that are my walks in the coulees, by the rivers amongst pheasant and deer and ice floes in spring. Stories that are my pilgrimages to prairie shacks lived in by my people, by me. This is me picking foxtails and lying by the side of the road. These are my stories, our stories.

They will become the bones to hold me, the wind to lift me, my leaps of faith.

At the Amigo Motel in Harvey, North Dakota, where they can't for the life of them connect me with a long distance operator, and where I find someone else's shoes under the chair in my room, but where they load me up with fresh-picked cucumbers in the morning, and I can dip the cucumbers in the salt I've poured on my dashboard, where there are hollyhocks outside the front door and where the bedspread in my room is a home-made quilt, and the cupboards are full of pots and pans and salt and pepper shakers, and there's an old gas stove and big porcelain sink and a fridge, and a string to the light bulb in the bathroom, and a flowered oilcloth on the table, I'm happy, like a kid exploring a favourite lake cabin.

I HAD A GREAT AUNT NAMED ALBERTA

By the time I reach Minnesota I'm tired from three days of driving. Time to think and listen to music has given way to backache and tiredness. And while I can't stand people who claim the prairies are boring, I will admit my dog and I have had it by the end of North Dakota. My parents and nieces meet me at the family lake cabin in Minnesota. Mum puts the scallops in the freezer for me. Maggie with her long ponytail, and Erin with her short hair, haul me immediately to the water before Dad can show me the garden. My mother joins us too, her Australian crawl steady and even next to Maggie, who hops up and down to prove she can "go under," and the emerging power of Erin's butterfly stroke. Me, I learn I can "stay under" longest.

I thought about taking the scallops out for supper, but I decide not to, and no one pushes the issue. Maybe later. That night, we play cards and sit at the round kitchen table going over the old stories from the family photo album, a huge book, perhaps two feet by two and a half, full of photos of rivers and tornadoes, grandparents by old cars, picket-fenced houses in Winnipeg, great aunts with names like Netta and Alberta, photos with serrated edges. There are endless pictures, in black and white, of babies being bathed in porcelain sinks.

You kids always liked tornadoes, my mother says. You liked blizzards, too. We could hardly get you all inside. You didn't want to miss anything.

I smile as she says this, and remember that even as an adult visiting this cabin I would cheer for the tornado to be a good one, so we could huddle in the basement, a family again, making forays for food and blankets, building blanket forts while listening to far-off sirens and the terse and contradictory reports on a battery-operated radio....

I am old enough now to know that a tornado is a disaster that threw garages in the air, terrorized, maimed, and flooded. I am old enough now to know it is more than that. I am old enough to understand that tornadoes are our way to cast and recast reality.

I know a tornado is how we staked our place, how we were never so alive, how we found our rock-bottom place of faith and laughter in the turbulence. How we learned to say, Yes, yes! as the tornado swept through. It's how we learned to behave for the rest of our lives. It's our marker and our badge.

It is the parade of cars only nature could organize, driving down streets later, when it is all over, to see whose home is cut in half, the toilet and sink of a perfectly sliced home exposed for us all to see, like a doll house. Prairie modesty forgives this moment.

It is watching our big sister Judy, in the theatre basement chaperoning younger sister Donna's birthday party, and all the adults we don't know wailing and whining, and Judy saying, Grow up, there's kids here, and us cheering on our big sister, Yea, Judy! while the toilets back up all over the floors, and those adults get subdued and resentful, and us kids snigger and can hardly wait to get outside to see the chaos.

It is Mum, or Dad, driving through streets with water over the wheel wells, to rescue us from the theatre, the old Chevy wagon turned into a boat, and all us kids laughing and weighing it down further.

It is hail the size of softballs, in the cold after the tornado, destroying the big greenhouse next door, every year knocking out hundreds of panes, and each kid stores the biggest hailstone in the freezer to compare, running to meet each other barefoot over broken oak limbs and acorns.

It is my brother Brian disappearing from the basement as the storm, in front of our eyes, sheers off the overhang of our house, as if it were an unwanted seam allowance, and Brian, freckle-faced boy, reappears with the Oreos to keep us from starvation and fear.

It is my mother grabbing my brother Andy and running with him in her arms when oak branches crash down around him like the tines of a tuning fork or a wishbone.

It is my father pounding at the door in the storm, Let me in, let me in, and my girlfriend and me yelling in caution, as we were taught to do, Who is it? Then understanding the power we are all facing and using our girl strength to haul open the door against the suction.

It is a piece of straw stuck straight, like a needle into the oak tree, force so true it went to the heart.

At the Minnesota State Fair with my sister Judy, we sit in the shade eating deep-fried cheese curds. We listen to an old-fashioned band with five violins, an accordion, and drums. They play polkas, and love songs to twirl around in, and then more polkas to make you light-hearted. They're polite and fun like on Lawrence Welk. We visit the 4-H barns and the art fair. When we're tired, we simply sit and watch a giant tank of big-mouthed bass. It is soothing just to sit on benches, eating deep-fried cauliflower, watching the big-mouthed bass, with all the other people sitting watching them, too. As my sister and I walk and talk and eat, we meet politicians she works with, friends she knows. We're alike in this, my big sister and me. Politics and friends.

There is one booth promoting the production and consumption of buffalo meat, the animals strong, perfect with the prairie, as they always were.

There is a homemade video of a buffalo out on the bare plains giving birth. It is unedited video, and as the buffalo labours long and hard, women begin to gather before the television screen, as crowds surge by behind us. It is as if we, like the buffalo on the screen who gather around to help her, are her labour coaches. As we begin to breathe in unison, to push with her, a man – whose wife is amongst us – tells us that the buffalo is in no pain. We turn on him in unison, stare him down, then stand, pushing with her, until the baby's head, already engaged, crowns, and she delivers.

I go to join the children looking at a female buffalo, a real one who stands quietly in her enclosure. We can touch her. I get to bury my hands in her heavy mane, sink them deep into the curled and heavy coat. She is alive and solid and her coat is deep. Oh. Oh. I want to curl up with her.

A Minnesota farmer paid for your birth, my mother tells me.

When you were born, we were Canadians living in Minnesota, she says. I asked the doctor if he'd come out to the house. *Out*, he said in the way people like to try on our accent. And then he said the word *house* like that, too.

Yes, Canada, I will come *out* to the *house*.

And he declared he would not bill us for the cost of your birth. That, he said, would be covered by the next rich Minnesota farmer who walked through his door.

Is that true, Mum?

Yes, that is a fact.

EVERYTHING HAPPENED WHEN I WAS TEN

My mother once said, as the stories kept running into each other, Everything happened when I was ten, because everything did happen then, or that's when she got the story and remembered it.

When she was ten and living in Winnipeg, she lost both her grandmothers. One moved to New Zealand and became a bigamist, and one died. She got to see the dead one out in Ontario.

I asked if she saw buffalo, but she said no, they were dead and gone by then.

My mother wants me to see the house where this dead grandmother was waked. We've driven from Minnesota to Comber in southern Ontario for the family reunion. The hotel Mum's booked is in Comber, the same place as her reunion, and she's happy how that will work so well. We can walk and talk, visit and explore.

Only we arrive and there isn't any hotel in Comber. In the office of the car dealership where we stop to ask directions, my mother feels stupid and afraid, like she's got Alzheimer's or something, and that's not a worn out joke. Her brother Ernie just died from Alzheimer's in Winnipeg. I can hear her breathing funny, and saying all her brothers have died since the previous reunion, this could be her last one, and she was so sure we'd be staying here. She'd had the picture in her head for five months since she booked the rooms, that we'd be here where her grandparents and father had lived.

All four of the people working at the car lot come from the back rooms to the front counter to talk to her, help her make phone calls, and one woman even cocks her head and says she may have heard of Mum's family's name.

Then we're back outside amidst all the cars. Do you know how bereft you can feel standing in a car lot not knowing where you are going? All that promise of travel and you're immobilized? Mum isn't even certain where her family's house is. It's almost six decades since she's been here. She thinks we can learn things about our family the way she did in Ireland – stay in a place and meet people and have a beer with them and tell each other stories or lies about family history. She even envisions it like the Irish family who invited my family into their kitchen to lift glasses of home-brewed poteen and Mum and her 47th cousin stood ruddy-faced and stocky in the doorway, every inch of them related, or not even caring if they weren't related because they liked each other anyway.

I'm holding her hand, my brazen strong mother who I've seen stare down school boards, cause panic and consternation amongst the forces of oppression, stride through swollen rivers or tornadoes to grab her child from being swept away. My mother stands shrunken and crying.

An old man walks into the parking lot, headed for the office. He is her age or older. She releases my hand. I hold my breath and stand still. I swear I feel plates of earth lurching beneath my feet, as generations of knowledge and understanding shift and slide. She steps in front of him. Do you know the Hallatts? she asks. The brick yard Hallatts? he answers, and I feel my chest swell the way parents do when their kids, all falling apart and afraid, come on stage and make them so proud.

Their house was near a store, she says. Yes, he says, and points to a house two blocks away. They smile at each other, and it is a code from which I will be excluded, until I too am that age. When we pull up beside the brick house, lived in, full of life, still with the high and broad front steps, and with a balcony and porch now on the back, we know it is a house with children. Alive.

Mum says, relieved but with some mix of reluctance and shyness, the aftermath of emotion and shame, that there isn't time now to stop, that we'll come back after the reunion in a few days. No Mum, I say, we have time now. Because, somehow for me, this is the reunion. And we get out three cameras, three, because there have been too many disasters before. Jammed film, dead batteries, lost stories. Now we have three sets of the pictures, Mum on the front steps, Mum and me on the front steps, view from the side street, view from the back.

She stands firmly on the sidewalk, as if she has found her base again. As if for some moments she'd been homeless, as if the tornado had swept away the child. Gone.

She points to the bay window.

That's the room, she tells me. That's the room where my grandmother was laid out. It happened when I was ten.

It's odd — much later, months after this visit to Comber, I dream we are trying to bring one of our grandmothers back to life. This is a secret of my mother and sisters and me. Until we are sure we can do it, we will keep her hidden. We keep taking her temperature, like bringing back someone from hypothermia. She keeps growing warmer, and we keep looking at each other. Eventually I take her to a hotel with me. None of the staff can see her, except they can see a cup when she holds it, like in an old movie about ghosts. She keeps growing younger as we try to figure out what we're doing. She has become a girl by now. When I take her upstairs in the hotel, I am waylaid by a political acquaintance who says, Let's talk. We go into a basement hall. Usually we avoid each other. Now he wants a discussion. Usually I listen. This time I tell him he's wrong. I leave and walk up the staircase. I am naked except for a short cardigan. I have to look for my grandmother. She has become my niece. She is becoming too young. She is too confused here alone and doesn't understand why I abandoned her to talk to the man in the basement.

My mother points to the bay window: I came on the train to Comber to see this grandmother I'd never met. I was ten.

(I get right into this, and oddly, I have no concept of who this grandmother is in my history. She would be my great grandmother, I translate in my head, as if practicing a rusted form of race algebra. I feel as if I am rehearsing at being a human being, having a family history.)

That's the room where they laid her out, she says as she points to the window. Everyone came and went to see her and visit each other around her body or out in the kitchen.

There were six windows forming the bay, big enough for her coffin, she says. She was a big woman, but then I was ten and everyone looked big to me. I'd never seen my grandmother before, except the picture of her on our living room wall in Winnipeg, and I'd never seen anyone dead before. She was said to be kind, firm, and religious, and she looked very stern. Just saying her name aloud is enough to put the rod up your spine. Ann Jones Hempstock Hallatt. Her hair was grey and pulled back in a knot. I was alone in that room with her. I was scared and fascinated. Instead of running I stood and stared. In my mind she looked strong enough to come back from whatever was doing this to her. I stared and stared. Do you know what it's like? You stare so long that things start to move?

To this day, I swear I saw her breathe.

I ran screaming. She's breathing! She's breathing! All these stony-faced Hallatts set down their tea and strode in to look at her.

She wasn't breathing.

My mother takes my hand and leads me along the walk. Out in the backyard there, she points, that's where all my cousins played. There was this kid next door. Every day during the week of the funeral he beat up all my cousins. He was a nasty, nasty bully. I was a real tomboy, says my mum, and I smile because I don't know of any of us in this branch of the family who aren't, and pretty strong, too. I'd had enough with this kid, she says. One day I beat the living stars out of him. He went home crying, A girl hit me, a girl hit me!

Oh thank God yes, this is my mother, conquering bad guys, bullies, creeps.

Later I understand how badly I want things snapped back into this proper alignment, like at the eye doctor when the red tractor in the golden field suddenly regains its sharp edges, and you feel your world is fixable after all.

And then the best thing happens. Mum wonders aloud if she should go to the door, and I say, Go ahead, try it. I stay back, thinking maybe she'll have more luck alone.

She walks up the stone steps, knocks softly. A teenage girl comes to the door. She's the babysitter. Does she go all weird and suspicious when this total stranger, when this woman, my mother, says, Excuse me, but this was my family home and I haven't been here for 65 years and that's the room where my grandmother was laid out and could I just look in, I've come so far? Does this girl panic and slam the door? Does she act like some street-proofed zombie who would never dare look into someone's eyes, or talk to a stranger on the train, or use some common sense and human kindness? Does she turn away my mother? No. That blessed girl looks into her eyes, and I would bet you everything I own that she saw a woman who needed to come home. And she said, Yes, please come in.

At the reunion, I'm glad I'm with my mother. My mother's name is Erin, but she was born Edna Mae and mostly people here at the reunion call her Mae or Mamie. I'm the only kid who could come with her this time. Since the last reunion, all three of her brothers have died. Her parents have been gone for years. She's the last of her immediate family. It doesn't matter how old you are, she says, it still hurts to lose everyone.

Mostly I feel disconnected at this reunion. By and large, the women like me, and the men don't. I refuse to sit, as the men tell the women to do, for the family photo, so all the men can stand behind us. Women sitting, hands folded in laps, men standing over us. Screw that, I think. Before the men can assume their positions, I walk to the place behind my mother, who sits in a chair before me, and put my hands on her shoulders, and she reaches her hands back to touch mine. We both know no one would have the nerve, even in this family, to challenge this combination of my mother and me. Soon more women stand on either side of me, whispering their thanks, as if we have just declared rebellion, and we have.

She tells me later that her Ontario cousins confessed they were always intimidated by the Manitoba Hallatts – had had it pounded into them that only the Manitoba branch of the family worked for a living. And in turn the Manitobans were intimidated by the wealth of their Ontario cousins. That class thing, she says, carries on to this day.

I tell off an uncle who never gets told off, after he yells repeatedly at someone from the stage where he stands with all the older generation. He hollers over and over at someone down on the floor about how to operate his camera. I look around to see who he is insulting, and realize finally that he is yelling at me. But I am not using his camera. I am using my mother's camera, taking pictures for her. Something rises quickly in me, and I yell back at him as loudly as he has yelled at me, and his children choke with laughter.

In all the family group shots, where the people hold up placards identifying the family grouping, they only list the name of the patriarch, this side of the family, mostly, being composed of males. Mum and I always take a big marker, and next to her father's name, Nick, add her mother's name, Georgina. It's all kind of funny, as if we're some kind of oddball comedy team, but kind of sad, too.

When they call out the roll of who has died since the last gathering, I have never seen my mother so lonely, so beautiful in the way people are when they are trying to maintain dignity and the tears fill their eyes, so knowing that they are the last ones who know the stories.

My mother is strong and energetic, and in this we're alike, but on this trip she's having trouble with diverticulitis. It's an intestinal problem that's painful and unpredictable, and it pisses her off.

One day she'll be sitting by the Atlantic, a lobster sandwich in her hand, huge smile on her face, red hair flying, pant legs hiked up from splashing through the water.

Another day she'll be shivering beneath blankets, and I will feel all a person can feel while watching her parent suffer. Perhaps this intensity, as sporadic as it was in the six weeks of travel, made all the days more intense. Only looking back can I see that. When you're in it, you are too occupied with the needs of the moment to understand any bigger pattern. You only know the motel is too full, or too expensive, or we've gone too long without eating, or the windshield wipers need replacing. She has told me stories all the way across the country, but it is in Cape Breton, I realize, that for both of us the stories start to change. From the everyday to the myth. As if we are given permission, the closer we get to the ocean where our ancestors came across, the further we are from our everyday homes. Maybe I am using Cape Breton as a stereotype, I don't know. Or perhaps we all need some place to go as far away from home as we will get. Or it is simply that after so many thousands of kilometres, my mother can really tell her stories, when we are not busy with maps seeking the right exit near Sydney, or when the cramps are not seizing her face with pain. And it is in Cape Breton the stories can begin to become mine, as if some transference takes place, the link forged.

The stories will be repeated on the way back home across Canada when we miss the turn at North Bay and end up long and winding, like the stories, on the road north to Temiscaming, as if we need to get off the track before the convolutions can begin.

There are times in the telling when I am like a child she is tucking in, and I want to hear the same story over and over. Just to hear her voice. There are other times when she tires and grows old, and I am the one who puts the blanket on her.

It's as if in the everyday there are too many chores, too much busyness, even for the retired, as if we both need miles below the feet, long rolling stretches to loosen the tongue. As if the highway is taking us back to the places of the stories, as if the road were our own place, where no other lives demanded, or took their share. Stories to be told to me this first and only time in her 75 years. Not that they are secrets, but it's as if before they never seemed worth the telling, as if other voices, causes, meetings, other people's songs were more worth the singing; or the rotations were wrong, as if the wheels beneath us were the only rhythm to release the words again.

My mother has become my narrative link, the starting point, the mid-point, the link between stories lost and stories passed forward.

When I stayed a long time in Nova Scotia those few years ago, I began to see stories and understand them, not as the constructs of a journalist, but as everyday ways of seeing and continuing. It was as if I emptied out and refilled myself – shifted stories that I wrote from those researched and written for newspaper, or hard clips of 30-second voices for radio, slicing and editing tape late in the night to get the story on early – shifted them to stories heard in long repeated phrases, or part sentences said while driving. Before, as a reporter or traveller, I heard other people's stories. Now my mother and I are telling our own, while slowing down to admire a field of wheat, a lane of maples, a cemetery and church, long coastlines. And I wonder if this is our old prairie way, of standing side by side, eyes to the horizon, and beginning the narration.

Many times our stories start while looking out at the horizon, or the road, side by side, eyes ahead, stories halting, with silences and wind. Stories told just this once, like the first reading of a play. I hope I'm giving them breath and warmth, and that someday my nieces and nephews will add yeast and flour, get their hands doughy in them.

In the Maritimes I admired people and families who had lived one place so many hundreds of years, gravestones telling of their exact place on the earth. I admired how a story of a life or death would be told over and over until everyone knew of it.

It is as if it takes generations after major shifts occur before a member of a family slips into the role of writing its stories. As if the job, the job for me anyway, is not to have children, make more family, but to take the time to listen, and travel, and stand at buffalo jumps until the stories can be heard. And then the role is to write them down. And that is what I will do.

We are going to places where these stories make sense, the places they happened, or where they tie back centuries to relatives we hardly knew – where seeing a strange but familiar name in an old museum leads to wondering and asking, and where hearing the stories of United Empire Loyalists, or watching the French stepdancing in Cape Breton, takes my mother back to Ireland, births and movements and deaths, and wondering, when looking at a picture of someone maybe 20th generation removed, if we could be related. We hear music that calls back some kind of race memory, and it could be love or revulsion, bagpipes bringing tears or a smart rebuke about all the whining pipes in Brandon agricultural exhibitions, cows and horses and dung and pipes.

As if we belong to each little piece of the country – to the Ontario bricks her grandfather made, to the United Empire Loyalists in the Maritimes, to the river valleys of southern Manitoba, to train trips and love affairs – and we're finally seeing our country together through our own eyes.

Back home in BC, I would marvel how the Doukhobour people would time travel in conversations, one minute be in the present, and with no perceivable lurch of gears, be back in 1932, or 1895. Now my mother and I are doing the same.

In any conversation, she'll toss in some date from Manitoba history, or the way they pronounced Cabot as Cabo, with a long o, or a fact about Riel. It's as if all these years of living apart, I haven't had her stories, just a few, and I had to keep making my own. Or she'll drop it that in 1919 her dad, Nick, was on strike in Winnipeg. And I will say: Gramp was in the Winnipeg General Strike? And there it is, the penny dropped, her father was part of a history so big we still remember it. Or the year of her birth, 1918, they all nearly died during the influenza, on the godforsaken farm.

How could I not have known.

How could I not have known these stories.

When Judy was born, she starts – your father was exploring on Hudson Bay....

I love the birth stories. They're as reliable as teddy bears, as strong as the log houses we built on our living room floor. I conjure the Mackenzie Expedition, snow-blinded eyes, dogs dropping from exhaustion, shrieking blizzards.

This was 1945, she says. They would be away for months. The only communication would be through a Hudson's Bay post, or through a supply plane. He wasn't in Winnipeg when Judy was born.

When I wonder how he could be so far away, she says

back then dads weren't expected or allowed to be there for births. They were out earning a living.

Your father couldn't be expected to leave the expedition and wait around at the hospital, she says.

Besides, she says, and there's a twinkle in her eye, a good friend of ours, whose own wife was in hospital having their baby, took me to the hospital. And he came to visit and bring flowers after he'd been down the hall seeing his own wife and baby.

And though my mother speaks practically of the times and the customs, of fathers away working, I have to say she enjoyed the uproar and the way my dad came running.

Here's how it goes:

The signal will be sent through the botanical expedition. They're far out on the tundra, mapping flora and fauna and the way shorelines grow in, and the Indian guide is to receive the message from the pilot of the supply plane, and relay it to our father. He's to wave with one arm, a casual "all's well" out onto the tundra if it's a good birth, and wave both arms if something's wrong and Dad should come back by bush plane. Do you have that? One arm good, two arms bad?

We know how this story must go. The mistake is made somewhere along the communications line; the guide is asked to wave with both arms if the news is good, and he does, signalling to my father that all is well, first-born and mother are happy. From the far off camp, my father sees the bush plane land, and the guide jumping up and down waving both arms like cranked up semaphores.

This is like a bedroom farce, where one character enters as the other exits and messages are confused. If it were on stage, like our high school version of *She Stoops to Conquer*, doors would be slamming and the entire set of the tundra would rattle.

My father shoves off in the canoe, hauls up to the plane and takes off for Winnipeg and the hospital, rushing bearded and khaki-clad down white corridors.

My mother takes a certain glee in this next part.

The nurses bar him entry. They believe the other man, the one who brought the flowers and chocolate, is the husband. My father is distraught, my mother and the baby, Judy, are calm throughout.

The birth stories always start out, When you were born, or, When Judy was born... They are our beginnings, our stories, our mother's stories usually, the first story telling, as reliable and nourishing as porridge. It's a cruel censure that so quickly rubs out mother stories, as if they were not worth the telling or the space they take, the story so often untold, whisked into another room, like eraser filings brushed from the page.

Sometimes mother stories are difficult. It takes time

before they can be told. Like the one about my sister Donna who tried so hard to have more babies, because her first died in Winnipeg a month after being born. Then many years later a foetus she carried was dead a few months after conception, and the doctor wanted her to carry it to term and go into regular labour.

Only after fierce argument would the doctor relent and agree to a D & C instead. He told my sister to put on a hospital gown, told the orderlies to wheel her into the operating room. They wheeled her there, then left her alone to wait. No one, they said, could do a D & C for hours, and then they walked away.

Mum can't finish this story right now – her eyes fill up with tears and anger, and we put it aside, one of those times where you set down the story as if it were a skein of yarn or a book.

Sometimes on this trip we take wrong turns, though rarely. The roads across Canada are familiar to me. But we could be talking or we could be tired, and there might be a detour. Or a sign we miss in the clutter of small town signs where everyone who lives there knows the way anyhow. Once we're out of town, my road-tired mind will jar with questions that pop to the surface like batter in hot soup. I'll say, How did that one go again? How did you get your name?

It was 1918, my mother says, the year of the big flu.

She talks about the big flu as if it is part of our common knowledge, like the Winnipeg General Strike, like how to shovel snow or pick off woodticks. But I don't know about the epidemic until this story.

The story, and the flu, too, starts when she's being born, November, on the hillside in the Pembina River Valley of southern Manitoba, near La Rivière. The name as I've heard it is not *la rivière*, as if it sounded as French as it looks, the river, but lare-i-veer, with the accent on lare.

For once Gramp is home from the railway, because he's dying from the flu.

He's come in at the CPR depot. There is no one there to meet him, and he doesn't expect anyone. It's November, and somehow he gets up that hill. Later, some people come up the snowy hillside to stand outside the house to pay their respects. The men remove their hats for a moment, the women leave a pot of soup. They don't come inside. By now everyone has had someone die from this flu.

Nana looks up to see him when he comes in. There is everything to be said. There isn't much to say. She is going into labour, and he is dying. The death of their last baby, William, in Winnipeg, hangs between them. Nana had agreed to leave the city after he died, to go into the countryside to start over. Death and birth mix up in the same room, the memories and reality. Their three boys, all under the age of ten, try not to make too much noise, but their stillness only emphasizes Nana's heavy labouring, Gramp's laboured breathing, and the silence of the snow.

There is a pounding on the door. One of the boys runs to answer it. At least it's something he can do. A large woman stands framed by the log walls and the snowbanks and the wind. They don't know her, nor she them. She looks at the room, at them, closes the door against the wind, and removes her coat. To hell with this town, she says. You need help.

My name is Edna Mae Grady, she says.

She nurses Gramp back to life. She helps Nana deliver my mother into life. She says, This baby will have my name. Then Edna Mae Grady leaves the prairie shack, and the baby, duly named Edna Mae, lives and thrives and runs through ravines and goes to school, and then she grows up and goes to work at The Hudson's Bay store in Winnipeg.

My mother's told me stories before of working at The Bay. I'm certain she worked in the scarf department. This is how I think of The Bay, with a scarf department.

She would tell me that Christmas was such a wonder – "so grand" would be her actual words – with the store decorated to the high ceilings, and people rushing in and out blowing their hands from the cold, and fur coats on all the women, like the kind Nana finally got and I have it to this day (and woe to the person who tells me I shouldn't wear my Nana's fur). And the hats the women wore, and the hats the men wore. I have those pictures, too, Nana and Gramp striding down Winnipeg streets. You can see the puffs of breath coming from their mouths, because the exciting pictures to me are of the cold, not the summer ones where no one is brisk.

But the other thing at The Bay – and it probably wouldn't be allowed now, and who could imagine it anyway because there's hardly any ceremony left in a department store, but this is how Mum described it. The stairs are wide and magnificent, coming right down from the mezzanine to the middle of the main floor with a wide flourish to the main doors. The aisles aren't smashed in by racks of clothes. No, there is room to breathe, like the prairies themselves. A wide sweep. There are real musicians and the people stop in their shopping, because this is Christmas at The Bay, and this is special and they have come here for it, not just some person yelling "Christmas Special" through a crummy public address system, and everyone is bedraggled.

Up on the mezzanine there is a chandelier, and don't forget the tree, my God, it must be 30 feet high, a huge spruce, and lit with real candles! And everyone looks up, and the orchestra begins, and they lift high the roast suckling pig with an apple in its mouth, and on a silver platter they carry it in ceremony, down, each step taken carefully, because the pig is heavy, and this is Christmas at The Bay.

And there is my mother, working at her counter. She is very beautiful. Her hair is swept up in a lovely clasp. She is trim and strong. She is a skater, a racing skater with long blades, and her face shows the colour of a young woman who loves cold and wind and ice. A very large woman selects a scarf and presents my mother with a cheque for her merchandise. My mother looks at the name on the cheque, then lifts her eyes and says, You are Edna Mae Grady and I am named after you. I'm your namesake.

Edna Mae Grady looks my mother over, and says with some dismay, And you were such a beautiful baby, and leaves the store.

This ending leaves me stupid. She said what? I ask as if I haven't heard. My mother just laughs, but this episode pricks at me. Maybe time has made it funny, and what is the point of caring even if it did seem strange? But a generation later, I am struck afresh by the rudeness, the inability to marvel at the wonderful circumstance of meeting in the scarf department in the midst of a lavish Christmas celebration, when last you met at childbirth in a log shack in a snowstorm.

Maybe Edna Mae Grady always made abrupt decisions, abrupt remarks. Perhaps she was sick of Christmas shopping, even at The Bay, and the pound cake in her bag felt like many pounds, and her feet ached. Maybe she was in the habit of saving or letting go of many lives, and her brusqueness was her armour, her safety vest.

Maybe later she regretted her remark.

Before this I was never sure why my mother changed her name from Edna Mae to Erin. But I'd never heard this story before, either. I think my mother didn't want to be named after Edna Mae Grady because Edna Mae Grady demanded it, even if she did save their lives. It's too much like Rumpelstiltskin, I expect. Maybe Edna Mae Grady's brusqueness and my mother's decision to change her name was the only way they could cut their strange cord. As if such sentimentality could not withstand the cold.

But there is some way that my mother is a true namesake, because I know in my lifetime I have heard the words of Edna Mae Grady come from her mouth. I know my mother, at 5'3", has also towered in doorways, been abrupt and imposing.

To hell with this town, I can hear these words coming from my mother, as she stands in a doorway making her decision, then strides in. Those words she heard as she emerged from the womb, the words from the big nurse standing at their door, which had to have rung now and then through my mother's life each time she had to buck up her courage. To hell with this town. You need help.

I always thought buffalo were male. Not all of them, of course, you needed the females to breed. But buffalo meant male. Bear meant male, except for females protecting their cubs. Most of the bears I've butchered were male.

When I started reading about buffalo, and dreaming them, they started to become female. I read in a book that it was the female buffalo who led the herds. That seems strange, I thought. And then I saw the same information again at the interpretive centre in Alberta, even heard an old woman near me read it out loud to her husband, loud enough so he could not miss it. And then I read in a book that smart old native women were considered to have buffalo wisdom. And that mostly the male buffalo lived alone. Somehow I always thought the males protected the herd, turning their powerful shoulders to the threat. But I was wrong.

Imagine living on that hillside in La Rivière, my mother says as we drive along past more rivers and hills. All Nana had there was her women's group.

When she says "women's group," I almost shake my head, as if the term can't belong to women before my time. Then I think, my God, Nellie McClung lived and taught right down the road in Manitou. Her politics were forged from the kind of isolation women like Nana lived in. My mother is telling me a story, and my mind is reeling with the knowledge that we fit into a bigger history.

As Mum tells it, they were young women and had

been on the farm too long. They were the wild women of La Rivière. Nana wasn't "Nana" then. She was Georgina, and she went by Jo.

Nana and these women are huddled in the night amidst the kerosene lamps, they didn't have electricity then, at least I imagine they didn't there on that "godforsaken hillside," as I have come to know it. They're playing cards, whist, like bridge with no bidding.

The men in the town know the women are playing cards tonight. A woman glances up from her cards; she is holding hearts, a lot of them, queen high. Where is the king, she wonders, and who has the ace?

A man looks in the window. This is true. We know this is a fact. We are not certain of the exact date, because sometimes Nana could embellish a story, but it is "the deepest of winter." So we will say it is January, a deep Manitoba January, with early dark and darker winds, and the women are deep under the light – let's make it an overhead kerosene chandelier – I know this kind exists because I have seen one in Nova Scotia. The chandelier, six small lamps on a wagon wheel, is lowered on a pulley, just above the women's heads. All the man at the window can see is the sweep of their hair, and the concentration in their shoulders as they lean into the light and the secrets of their cards.

They are young mothers. They somehow have left their children with their husbands and have this night alone playing cards. Or no, perhaps the children of all the women are in the one room in this house, settled side by side like cordwood in the one bed, under homemade quilts.

Okay. The kids are sleeping, the women are concentrating.

Nana hears a sound outside. She looks to the glass, the older ripply kind that wavers and distorts.

A man is watching them through the window.

The women, there are five or six, leave the table. Quickly. They capture the man, the snow is deep and their numbers are greater. They strip him and douse him in water.

Right on, Nana! I am thinking, of course not really remembering for the moment of this outrageous image that it is the coldest and darkest night in January, and the killing it can do.

They thought it was hilarious, my mother says in a voice that conveys it was not, and her eyes are just a little dangerous.

Usually my mother and I share a motel room, and sometimes we get separate rooms just for a break. Tonight, alone at the bathroom mirror, I see Nana is looking at me. It's happening, I say, and give her a wink.

Really all I see is her mouth. My mouth. The small

vertical lines extending up from my lips are Nana's. It's the only daily reminder of a woman I really knew very little. There are few people left to say, She has her Nana's mouth, so I say it for them.

I got some of my Nana's dresses after she died – modern ones my mother had bought her, because Nana did like to be up to date. Except I don't really feel anything of Nana when I wear them. But when I first put on her Persian lamb coat with seal trim, the one she saved up for in Winnipeg and wore all her life after she left the farm, when I put my hand in the pocket and pulled out the storage receipt from 1983, I thought, Hello Nana. I'm in here now.

I think I am following the buffalo again. As they led settlers to water, they have begun to lead me, too, into the prairie. They are allowing me to breathe it and taste it. To see and hear clearly. They'll take me to the water and the hills of the Pembina River Valley where my mother and Nana lived. When I go back and take time, I will see the buffalo that were hidden to me before.

And in taking the time I will see and hear whispers of stories. The stories need time and nourishment. They need walking around and long draughts of water. They need bathing in a river. They need to be carried a while, like a child, and set in the sun and breeze. They need music and food.

As I go to sleep, I understand that I am following the

buffalo again. I find them standing by the stories waiting for me. They give me my breath again. They carry me across rivers until I am strong enough to swim by myself. They show me how to face down a storm. They are giving me a backbone, for bearing burdens or for charging and galloping and kicking up my heels in dust and snow.

There are not many left. They are going the way of the stories and I have to listen to them while I can.

I haven't actually seen any buffalo since Minnesota. Except for the ones at a Niagara amusement park. I think it's the worst part of the trip for us. Whales in small pools, fallow deer so tame and obnoxious they shove people around, tear off backpacks and scatter them around in their ceaseless begging for food, buffalo in an open corral with not one blade of grass, not one tree, having to shit and fuck and sleep in front of us for our benefit and amusement.

In spite of this, I think the trip's lifting my mother as much as me – she too is leaving behind what holds her down, how you hardly ever take a holiday in your own town, and you need to shrug the same old tired air off your shoulders. Even at this horrid park, we become sick with laughter, staggering off a ride where I have been scared witless with vertigo and speed, me going, Mum, I really don't like this! while she sits next to me going, Whee! alternating with, Honey, I wish there was something I could do to help.

The devil is in her in our gleeful selection of a roadside motel, of traipsing around trying to find a beer with our supper. It's there in the wax museum as she mugs for my camera, shaking her finger at Ronald Reagan, or inviting the Queen to tea. It's there in her grin like a demented devil bedecked in blue rain gear and soaked with spray amidst hundreds of tourists at Niagara Falls on the Maid of the Mist. The last time we brought you here, she says, you kids never looked up from your comic books.

We did, too, I said. I remember.

It startles me to learn how much my mother travelled back and forth across Canada when she was young, as if I were the only one who travelled, hitchhiking with girlfriends through my youth, or taking train trips and being met by relatives along the way. And I assumed, because of her attitude, that most mothers granted their daughters the same freedom, if we were sensible and careful. And if I found her attitude unusual, I just considered her more enlightened than other parents. Now I think she understood what I was doing because she'd done it herself. She was standing in the doorway watching me on my adventures, worrying some, but also trusting my instincts and her training.

Lowney's Nut Milk Chocolate Bars!
Peanuts! Popcorn!

Lowney's Nut Milk Chocolate Bars!
Peanuts! Popcorn!

I can see her walking onto a stage, trying her lines, turning round and round to peer into darkened corners, walking to the edge and looking down, then out over the seats, to test her new sureness alone.

*Low*ney's *Nut* Milk *Choc*olate Bars!

Lowney's Nut Milk Choc'late Bars!
*Pea*nuts! *Pop*corn!

Then she'll smile to herself, having gotten it right to her satisfaction, bow, and walk offstage.

Her scene is set. The rest is just detail, for this is what she best remembers – the porter calling that chant. And her performance is to call up the exact rhythm and cadence, while the wheels clack beneath her and my Nana, from Winnipeg west to Vancouver, and south to Seattle.

This trip to Seattle happened when I was 10, my mother says. Nana would have been 37. It was April, 1929.

Nana's sister lived in Seattle. This sister was sick, mostly sick of her husband. They'd just separated.

The photos of that train trip are neatly captioned

with white ink, in the hand of a careful observer. Each word is capitalized, inspiring in the reader a certain formality and emphasis:

> Taken From The
> Observation Car of a
> Moving Train
>
> Mount Stephen
> Field, BC
>
> Foothills of Canadian
> Rockies
>
> or
>
> KITSILANO BEACH
> BC

We took our sandwiches on the train – enough to last a few days, she says. The money we used for chocolate bars.

And then she does this thing to conjure up the porter, she squeezes her eyes hard tight shut and her tongue grips her bottom lip a moment, and she begins to chant like him, tentative at first and you can tell she hasn't got the rhythm and notes quite right.

Lowney's Nut Milk Chocolate Bars!
Peanuts! Popcorn!

And I ask her to do it again.

Her memories of the trip are of quirky smells, daring leaps, smart retorts, her ten-year-old body sure and strong enough to keep pace with her quick ten-year-old mind.

She remembers leaping for the train when it was moving, she remembers landing safely, she recalls her mother's terror and relief.

I don't know if Nana's seen the ocean in 25 years, she tells me, then begins imitating Nana, drawing huge draughts of air and puffing her bosom out like Sara Bernhardt:

Oh, Oh, The Ocean!

For Nana it was like coming home, Mum says, but for me home was the prairie, and I couldn't see the attraction. There's Nana getting all weepy and me thinking my God, it smells like a wet Airedale.

We got to Seattle and I met my American cousins. In her superior way, my older cousin lost no time in informing me that Nana's mother had become a bigamist. It was bad enough when she'd deserted my granddad in Winnipeg and moved to New Zealand. But we'd gotten used to it. But this cousin could hardly wait to inform me that my grandmother had just become a bigamist over in New Zealand. Can you imagine how we felt? Not only did we feel awful for granddad, and even though we were barely Catholics anymore, it seemed, I don't know, immodest or something to become a bigamist. But what really gored me was that we'd just left Winnipeg and hadn't heard a thing about it!

Listening to this, I'm smiling at the folklore and bravado, but it's also dawning on me that this story has some relation to my life. In this incidental way I'm learning about the women in my family who have left their husbands. My great grandmother? They did stuff like that then? It seems like a dust devil is having fun with history here. Small tornadoes like mirages twirling around on the prairie, rearranging patches of dirt, bouncing up and down and teasing with the promise of real trouble. I'm feeling inside and outside all at once, far inside a story and far away, having to twist my head and see things from a different angle.

My mother's still in Seattle seething at her cousin:

I was sure my cousin was making this up, just to have one over on me, even if I never liked that grandmother much. My cousin said I shouldn't tell my mother because it would upset her, and for a number of days I didn't. But I was just 10. And when my mother and I went for a walk, I told her about it.

She said this story was sheer foolishness, that her mother was Catholic and wouldn't remarry, and she went straight to her sister to put a stop to it. Except it was true.

As I listen to my mother, it isn't the bigamy that jolts me. It was just a legality, and an interesting twist on the times. But as I listen to all this I am mentally counting on my fingers. Okay, on my mother's side, that makes my great grandmother packing off for New Zealand. That's one. Two, a story I heard before, is about Nana packing up the kids and chickens at La Rivière and telling Gramp he can move to Winnipeg with her or stay and run the farm himself. Three is this aunt in Seattle. Four is the time my mother left Dad and us for a year in Brandon.

Mum's ready to get back on the train in Seattle:

We wanted to leave for Winnipeg right away. We wanted to be with granddad, and besides, this upset had somehow become a victory for my American cousin, and she was really lording it over me. Maybe she wanted me to hurt in some way, too, to level us out, since she was stinging from her own parents' separation. But our railway passes were for certain days and we were stuck in Seattle. Nana and I went for walks on the beach. We collected seaweed. We wrapped it in newspaper and put it in our suitcases to take back to Winnipeg – so Nana could still smell the ocean sometimes. Aunt Katie walked past our bedroom. What is that smell? she said. The seaweed was putrid. Just putrid, once you noticed. It made us feel naive and foolish and unfamiliar with the ways of the bigger world, and we returned to Winnipeg relieved to be home.

I have barely digested this as more than an anecdote, when the dust devil plays with me again. I learn from my father that his own grandmother, back in the early 1900s, left her drunken husband in Otterburne, another Manitoba town, and she, too, headed for Winnipeg to start her own boarding house, and he can even remember the address, 631 Furby. I am looking at my full hand, a full count of five women, two great grandmothers, one grandmother, one great aunt, my mother.

Did someone forget to write some history somewhere? Is my family really so bizarre?

And there were aunts who never married, who travelled to work as teachers in remote parts of Manitoba, like Bield and Friedenstall, and Cranbrook in BC Maybe even on the same train with the same porter calling his Lowney's Nut Milk call. I can hear the lure of the chocolate attending travel and romance. And I immediately chastise myself for romanticizing, am sure their lives weren't romantic, probably boring in lots of ways, with crummy living and working conditions. And again the dust devil dips its egg beater tail into my certainty and I think okay, maybe they were romantic. Maybe they, too, loved travel, the times alone in their rooms, reading or writing in their journals, or on the train, meeting new people. Maybe they liked being alone! The point is, they up and did it. Was this happening in every family, were women all over packing up and moving, not quite the traditional women we're led to believe? Would we know if we only asked the questions?

Is this what my mother always saw? That sometimes you have to pack up and go? Take your stand, make your leap?

We left the rancid seaweed in Seattle, she says. And then we got on that train and travelled! I got to hear the porter again, singing out his chant, and I got to look out the window and we took more pictures and Nana made sure I didn't take any more wild leaps for the train, and after a while it became sort of a secret joke between Nana and me. I don't think she ever told Gramp. And that's really what I prefer to remember of that trip: the pictures we took from the train window, how I leaped from the platform, and made it! And the chant of the porter: Lowney's Nut Milk Chocolate Bars.

I'm sitting here thinking, with all that travel and movement, alongside a girlfriend, her mother, or alone, that little tomboy leaping for the train or beating up a backyard bully, travelling cross-country, eager eyes taking it all in, feeling every rhythm in her young strong body,

and beside her, her mother who at the same age had travelled from the Isle of Wight to Scotland to Canada and
across the prairies to Manitoba, is there any doubt that
years later my mother could sing out with pure joy:
Lowney's Nut Milk Chocolate Bars, and that I, living
once more on my own, would be smiling with pure joy as
I write it down and begin to enjoy my travels alone?

SIREN CALLS

thought coming here to the Atlantic might be too hard, seeing my fisherman friend again. But he comes to see me immediately, and we talk a long time. Later he brings me scallops, a lot of them. Reparations, I call them, and the image makes me smile.

My brother Andy's veranda here in Freeport where my mother and I are sitting is like Nana's in Winnipeg, only far bigger. My mother and I have walked with the dogs to the Bay of Fundy in the wind, then hiked up to the hilltop cemetery. The dogs, mine and my brother's, are happily worn out and have taken to the old couches, circling round and round to mat up the old blankets.

We've come to know the people in the homes we can see. In our visits here before we have met their children, and we've met their grandparents. We know who has lost children, and which children were born later.

From my fisherman friend who lives down this hill, I have heard the story of the death of his young daughter many years ago. From my friend down the road, I have heard the story of the death of her baby boy. I know these children's names, have even visited their graves. Five years or twenty years after their deaths, their parents talk about them in a tone that is as ordinary as houses. They will trudge down the basement to dig into a supply of plastic flowers kept for regular grave tending. Their other kids know the stories, however tragic, the neighbours do, and so do casual acquaintances.

My mother tells me her story, our story, as if she were alive at the time, but I realize somewhere in the telling that she wasn't even born yet. I've begun to understand this of story tellers, how they seem to slip around in time and it's not deliberate. It's just as if they have the ability to be of a place, to slip in and out of someone's skin, or have that person slip into theirs.

It's the story about her little brother, who died before she was born. As I listen to my mother I think she calls him her little brother because she grew up and he didn't; over the years he became her little brother, and in some way she became his guardian. Or maybe she became the guardian of his story.

You know I had a little brother who died, says my

mother, as she looks out over the homes, out over the cove to the horizon.

You told me a long time ago, but I don't remember. I don't even know his name. Or any details.

His name was William, she says, and she closes her eyes and tells me this story, slowly, haltingly at first, as if the words are rusty. Or as if the short sentences were those recalled from childhood.

She begins to rock in her chair, as if trying for an easy memory.

William was born on St. Valentine's Day in 1914. He was the most good-looking child.

His hair was curly and blonde.

Boys wore little dresses then. He was Dad's angel. This was when we lived in Winnipeg. I wasn't born yet. I saw a picture of him.

She halts her rocking.

He died one year later, in 1915, on St. Valentine's Day, from pneumonia.

Born on St. Valentine's, died on St. Valentine's.

Nana was 24 years old. She told me years later that when she saw her baby had stopped breathing, and she knew he was dead, she did something that made her ashamed all her life.

My mother swallows. The years Nana's story was never told have compressed it. It is not a story Nana could ever embellish or enlarge in the telling. She just told the story, finally, once, to my mother. Mum is in Nana's voice again, only this time there is no puffed up bosom, no dramatics:

The boys were at school. Nick was away on the railway. William was dead and there was nothing I could do. I was alone with him. I ran out of the house. It was very cold, because it was Winnipeg in February. I hadn't a coat on, I just ran. And then I slowed down and walked. I walked into the store at the corner. The bell tinkled on the door, as it always did. I said hello to the man who ran the store, as if nothing was unusual, although he must have noticed I was without a coat. I bought myself a bar of chocolate. Then I said goodbye to him, and I left. I walked around the rest of the block, further and further from the house, eating the chocolate in the cold wind, and then I went back home. When I stepped into the warmth of the house, I could not believe what I had done. I had left my baby dead in his crib, and gone out in the cold and eaten chocolate. I must have been crazy. I picked him up and held him, and all I could think was, How could I have been so callous, so selfish?

Mum has stopped talking. I'm holding my arms crossed under my breasts, rocking in my straight-backed chair. It's quiet, with only the wind charging the house, and the sounds of the dogs breathing.

That's all, says my mother. She never told anyone else that story for all those years. She carried it so long without anyone ever telling her it was okay, or her analyzing it. I tried to erase her guilt. I told her she only did what she had to do to preserve her sanity.

Once on a trip here Mum pulled up an Atlantic pollock on the hand lines, hand over hand pulling and hollering. I have the picture of her on my fridge.

On that trip she wore my fishing union hat and a windbreaker, huge fish raised in one arm, and in the other hat swooping high, like a cowgirl who's just roped her first calf.

On this trip, it's as if everything breaks down, as if you can never do the same trip twice. Her body's breaking down, the boat broke down just on its way out of the breakwater, our day on the ocean gone and the only good thing is it broke down now, not on the first day of the lobster season. We all say this to each other, good thing it broke down now, not the first day of lobster. Thump. Clunk. How do you pick up again after being hauled back to the wharf by another boat, lunch bags, jackets, binoculars all hauled back up the ladder to flat ground?

As if our Sirens have rejected us, sent us back home to land and safety, as if an adventure denied is its own test.

What are our Sirens' calls? Our tinkers' bells? What calls us, taunts, entices? Calls us to the road, to fantasy and adventure? What keeps us going?

Thunder clouds and sheet lightning across a prairie sky, tornadoes twisting lifting stretching out like an unfurling braid, roaring like a train or a chimney fire. Atlantic waves thundering crashing, too big for anything but awe. Trains shrieking moaning, wind shaking the house, blizzard snow sifting in the windows, the huff and snort and whistle of a deer or elk passing the window, the bellow and shaking of earth of the passing buffalo. Northern lights, aurora borealis, seen on a prairie night, stop the car, turn off the lights, on your way home from a dance, listen to the whistle and whoosh and singing, and slowly, like a line of prairie dancers, put your arms across the shoulders of the aurora, and alone in the night, shuffle and bob and sway with the night sky.

Our siren song is backyard challenges, or clambering down rocks to the ocean water, fine music, fiddles and pipes, piano on the veranda, voices singing in harmonies so close you will shiver and cry and laugh all at once and know it can't get any better than this.

And what happens when my mother, my hero, slips a cog, when the siren call can't be answered, if even for a moment? When the hill can't be climbed, when she lies cold and drooling in her sleep, sick in a place too far from home, where I have taken her? When I leave her sleeping, and go try to find us some food, and can only find a cold submarine sandwich at the 7-11, thinking what in God's name have I done? Why have I dragged her here?

It is as if sometimes we are too much alike, we can't shrug off hurt, there are no shortcuts and we always have to go the long way, bump our ass over every rock, dig the grit from bloodied kneecaps, go all the way down before we can come back up again. And our only way is to know one day we'll make a story of it, to become actors a few moments in our own play, like children in a dress-up, to help us through, to play at bravado which makes bravery itself, and the only truth is to heed our siren calls and keep on going.

And then she wakes to whatever siren calls her, ready for adventure, a tour of the mine in Glace Bay, the embrace of the retired miner one year her junior, for the Men of the Deeps booming voices, for songs and rejoicing. She's been ready for adventure all along on this trip, even on The Maid of the Mist, for God's sake, ready for every tacky loud glittering neon bit of Niagara mist, for wax museums and tenting in the rain, historic forts, long days of travel, smoked fish and jerky, vodka and water, shared motel rooms and my dog at her bedside, for outdoor concerts on rain-drenched hillsides, for gritting her teeth and accepting help when it can't be helped.

Those are her siren calls, and I hope mine, for all that, and for simply keeping on.

So we're fierce to fish (as a friend would say), and that night, the night after the boat breaks down, we head for the wharf, and take turns casting our one line with mackerel bait growing soggy, fish and fish until the wharf lights go on, and cars stop by to see who's out here, and the ferry comes and goes, and I've gutted the small ones with an old pocket knife, holding them down on the cement kerbs, until Mum's cold and tired and ready for home, until I land a big one and she says, Okay kid, let me give that one more try.

The gravestones at Ingonish are marked exactly with the place on this earth or water of the person's life.

We stop by the big church at Ingonish in Cape Breton to walk through, to see the names on the tombstones. Each community has its own ways – some places with large trellises of white metal arcing over each stone, waiting for the wild roses to climb, a trellis made by the same business down the road that welds the metal lobster traps.

Some communities, like Brandon or Neepawa, relish stone angels.

At Ingonish we see stones with a small oval attached, like a locket, where when you're ready, when you've stood long enough listening to the water, imagining a life, you may step forward, open the locket, and the person will look out at you, this face in the locket forever protected from wind and rain.

At other stones, newer ones, we call out to each other, Mum, look! Honey, look! On one there is an engraving, a deeply etched line depicting the ocean, the cliffs and shoreline, lines drawing out where the man buried here – a man named Tom – took his boat each day to set his fishing net on the water. "Tom's net," it says on that spot on the engraving. He'll be remembered by his exact spot and his right to be on this earth and water.

My brother William didn't get a gravestone when he died, Mum says.

Dad – Gramp – couldn't stand living in that house in Winnipeg anymore. He wanted to get away from the house and its memories, so we moved – I say *we* moved, but I wasn't born yet – to the log cabin in La Rivière, on a hill of rock. There was not an inch of earth. Gramp went away to work on the railway, and Nana was left to cope with her three boys and this bloody shack on the hillside. Nana had only been 11 years old, a seamstress's assistant in Edinburgh, when her family moved to Winnipeg. She married at 16 in Winnipeg. What did she know of farming? Nothing. Gramp had wanted to move to the farm, and so they did. And then he was gone all the time. She had her women's group in La Rivière, and she had her three boys, and later she had me.

After ten years of trying, and too much loneliness and too much wind whistling through the walls on that godforsaken hillside, Nana made her decision. She could not stay there anymore for the sake of a dead child. She told Gramp if he wanted to leave the railway and run the farm, she would stay with him. If not, she was going back to Winnipeg. And she did. She packed up us kids and the chickens and moved to a neighbourhood where there were lots of families and a school close by, and she could cook on a decent stove and make enough for everyone in the neighbourhood if she wanted to, and play piano in the veranda while she watched us and all the other kids outside. She took a wood-turning class at a neighbourhood school and made frames for her petit point full of colours and concentration. And eventually, Gramp came back to Winnipeg, too.

The trip to Halifax by car takes three or four hours from Freeport. Mum says she came to Halifax once by train. I have no idea what she's talking about. I'm realizing more and more I have very little idea of my mother's life before children.

Edna Mae and her friend Mona Cove, they both had dads on the railway. Mona's family's all M's, it's the way things were done then. Mum can name them all off all these years later, by just saying, Wait, and then holding her breath with her head down and eyes shut and saying them fast without pausing like you do when it's right there out at the tongue-tip of your memory, Mona, Marion, Muriel,

Mac, Marie, and Marjorie.

She and Mona are skaters, and their school is General Wolfe Jr. High School in Winnipeg. All the girls in my mother's picture album wear white shirts and ties and v-neck sweaters and their hair is bobbed the same, shoulder-length, pinned back, each one smiling, arm-in-arm. Those girls, I can see them, moving from the picture, still arm-in-arm, and their hair begins to blow behind them, and they begin to stride, their worn black leather long-bladed skates cut through the wind and small whisks of snow at their feet, and like in a dance they let go their arms from each other, their horizontal caress releases to become a line of single girls, arms beginning to swing, hips and legs stride, and you can hear the cut of the ice, and the wind in their hair, and that is all.

Oh yes, they are railway girls and skaters. And my mother would be a writer. Mr. Arthur Hoole sits down by her in the school room after reading her story for the yearbook. You have it, you know. You must go on with this.

Edna Mae and Mona are 17 and school is out. They have only this summer left before they are 18 and too old for free passes on the railway. Each family has given their girl $25 and the addresses of relatives all the way from Winnipeg to Halifax.

Oh, the delicious pleasure, the delicious pressure to do

it now or never! To leave behind their part-time jobs at the scarf department of The Bay. To leave behind family gatherings at the Labour Centre, the small meetings of the CCF in their homes. To leave behind Nana's muffins and the family's boxer dog and the neighbourhood kids and just go.

I can hear Nana at the train station: Don't jump from any platforms! Remember! Have fun! Write! When the train is gone, she will turn away from the depot that so often claims her husband for his work, and now her only daughter, and she will say: Isn't that the limit? She will remember how she was younger than her daughter is now when she travelled across the Atlantic to Canada, still young when she married and had her first child.

She will breathe deeply, one deep breath, and go home to a house empty of children.

On the train, Edna Mae and Mona unpack sandwiches, arrange books and writing paper, then look out windows, stride the corridors, say hello to conductors and ticket takers, and even though they are independent girls on a long trip alone, they will tell everyone who their dads are.

On this trip they will find adventure, they will find huge lakes and the ocean and huge rocks, they will be wined and dined by rich relatives in far off Ontario, they will meet coal mining cousins in New Brunswick, they will see the warships in Halifax Harbour. Oh Winnipeg, soon you'll be far behind!

The rich relative greets them at the Toronto station,

and before taking them home explains how badly things have gone in the stock market crash. They've lost a lot, she explains, but doesn't want the girls to feel badly for them. The prairie girls look at each other, their dreams of luxury quickly swallowed, and instantly they are polite and ready for outhouses and cold water.

The home is a mansion – eight times bigger than anything they've seen. Three bathrooms and a huge dining room. The girls stare at each other bug-eyed, and enjoy every minute.

In Comber, she's telling Mona how they laid out her grandmother in the living room and how she beat up the backyard bully, and they're laughing, and meeting more relatives, and then back on the train to Montreal.

Nana's said there's a girl from near La Rivière? Manitou? Morden? who's singing at a hotel in Montreal, and they're determined to find her, and they do. They hear Dorothy Ault sing in the hotel's ballroom, and she invites them up to her room after the show, and she thrills them with stories of her concerts, her travels. She throws open a closet door to reveal beautiful clothes, and back on the train the girls are bug-eyed again, thinking, wow, what it would be like to be famous.

In Moncton they slow down; they meet two baseball players, members of the Moncton Beavers. They're baseball players who work in the mines. That's how it is, baseball players who work in the mines, not miners who play baseball. And Mona slows to a stop, foregoes the rest of the train trip so she can stay in New Brunswick with her Moncton Beaver.

But not Edna Mae. She has her ticket to Halifax gripped in her hand, and she plans to use it, all the way.

She gets back on that train and she goes, though she does not know one person in Nova Scotia.

The Halifax harbour! Where the year she was born, the same year as the great flu, when Gramp almost died, there was a whole other world going on. The Nimo hit the Mont Blanc and the Halifax water-front exploded. She remembers hearing of this. One thousand people killed, families losing as many as 25 members, and those not killed buried in wreckage and raging snow. This is history! This is Canada! This is a place she's never been!

The woman at Travellers' Aid in the station steers her firmly and kindly to the YWCA. A cousin of a friend tours her to Dartmouth and back. The next day he escorts her back to the train, through soldiers preparing for war, who whistle and yell, and scare her for the first and only time on her trip.

Sometimes on the train, she tells me, young men and women would sit up all night visiting, perfect strangers until that moment. Perfect strangers met on trains and corresponded for years after.

I may have been 18, she says, but I looked 14 or 15, and people kind of took care of me. Other railroad kids like me only got to go on trips with their parents. I never heard of any other girls who travelled alone.

I've never heard this story before. And to think I've made the same trip over and over now, not even knowing this was her route long before me.

It's as if we're discovering this mutual love of roaming, this thirst for the country. And later, too, far later, I realize there's more than tales here. There's rage that when we travel alone and rely on trust, we're called naive. As if trusting is not a skill. As if only fear has cachet.

I was heading west out of Winnipeg, I tell her. I'd already driven all the way from Nova Scotia. When I head back home, no matter what I say to the contrary, I can't seem to stop. It was September 12, a cold, blustery, Sunday – I remember the day, it was Andy's birthday and I should have called him in Nova Scotia – and I even thought about not leaving Winnipeg and my brother, Brian, because it was so nasty out. I was barrelling along as usual, and once again passed the exit for the Yellowhead, and the small sign saying that was the route to the Margaret Laurence house in Neepawa.

Another time, I said, then thought, When's another time? How many times have I said "another time" going by that Margaret Laurence sign? If it's not open today then I'm a fool and so what? Lord, it was cold, and even then I heard there's snow up in Dauphin.

In Neepawa, I found the house, which would open in an hour. An older man picking apples in the backyard said he lived next door, and he'd had a stroke, and their son said there was snow in Dauphin, and where had I come from, and he knew his wife would want me to come for coffee. Thank you, I said, I'd like to. But if the snow's coming, I better go get new wiper blades first, and I want to go see the stone angel, which I hadn't even known was real.

I stood in front of the stone angel, and I thought about Margaret Laurence, and stood in front of the gravestones of her and her mother, and then I got cold walking in the graveyard, and the snow was coming, and I drove back and knocked on the man's door.

A woman opens it and looks at me: My God, she says. He said you were 14, and driving across the country alone, and he said he asked you for coffee, and I said my God what on earth was her mother thinking letting her go off on her own like that at that age. Come in, come in from the cold.

In Glace Bay, I go knock on the door of the Will-Bridg House Bed and Breakfast even though the sign says check-in time is a few hours away at 4 p.m. Usually I can't stand people who think those signs don't apply to them, and just barge ahead, but today my mother is so doubled over in pain that I can't be thoughtful of anyone else. A woman in curlers comes to the door. Of course, she says, bring your mother in and let her lie down. Eileen Curry, she is, and a nurse as well. I don't think anyone could have been kinder to us at that moment, and two hours later Mum's ready for the underground mine tour, supper, and the Men of the Deeps. By the end of their concert, in the small hall with the big men and their history and their voices, we both feel stronger. We feel lifted by this place, connected by railway ties from the mines, to the railway of her father, or by age and the same politics she remembers from the Labour Hall in Winnipeg, by all these stories, songs of little towns and strikes and love and ties that lift us back to all the old countries we came from. We are strengthened by the warmth of people sitting close and singing and listening. By evening's end, the woman sitting next to us wants to exchange Christmas cards. The next day we go to the museum in downtown Glace Bay, and receive the same kind of welcome. Funny, at home in BC I used to welcome everyone, but most days now I don't want anyone coming to my door. I don't know what's gone wrong.

There were times on this trip with my mother that I would sit alone by the ocean and begin to hear the prairies. Both are like layers of music, the flute entering amidst the fiddles, a throb of bass picked out by deep listening, the things you don't see at first – textures of flattened wheat, back eddies in the river, cactus embedded ground level in the coulees, brown and cream and pink flowers after rain, trilobite imprinted on mother-of-pearl shells in the valley of the Oldman River.

In Cheticamp, Mum sleeps in the afternoon, her hand resting on Connor's head as he sleeps beside her. I have a long walk by myself. At the wharf a deckhand is alone on a large French boat from Des Isles de la Madeleine, the Magdalens. The wind is blowing, it's sunny, and we're alone out there by the boathouses and the water, him on his boat, me on the wharf. We hail each other and it's one of those flirtatious moments when neither of us speaks the other's language. At moments like these my French deserts me, and I search desperately for the word fish, all common sense gone, and 10 to 1, I'll bet, poisson became piscine, and I explain to him that down near Freeport, Il y a encore des piscines a pecher – There are still swimming pools to be caught. His English is as laughable as my French, and both of us gesticulate and laugh and talk louder and slower, reverting to our own language and laughing harder and harder as we each understand less and less.

I disturb my mother's sleep when I come back in from my adventures. She's still in that confused dream state, combined with the strain of the sickness. She's in the place we all go sometimes, where decades shift, and she needs to finish William's story for me.

William's grave wasn't marked – I think it was the times or how poor we were, she says, shifting herself up against the headboard.

Many years later, when we had all you kids, and lived by the Red River, it was so beautiful there. You kids had such freedom to roam. You'd run home to tell me about a deer or a fox or a racoon you'd seen. Everyone in the neighbourhood kept one eye out for everyone else's kids.

One morning I was washing dishes, looking ahead into the ripply glass we had for cupboard doors. I was conscious of this little blonde boy – his hair was curly – running into the house, but then it struck me a moment later that he was too young to be out on his own, and his mother would be worried to death. I looked for him. I called and called. There was no one there. Then I knew there never had been a child there. It was the little boy from the pictures I'd seen. It was my brother William. Your head tells you better, that there is a logical explanation. But there was no logic. It was him.

I wasn't scared. It didn't seem strange to me. I think it was the kind of place where he'd like to have lived. And it felt kind of good to be keeping an eye on him.

We all have our ways of remembering, she says. For me it was this way. For my brother, it was another. Before he died himself, my brother put a marker on William's grave.

Then my mother says, Let's go see some dancing.

And we do, we hit two pubs, watch step dancers and fiddlers and the piano player. I love how their hands range so fast and light and heavy. I could watch the piano player's hands as much as a dancer's feet. Mum can't drink right now because of the medication, but I can, and I make it a point to try out whatever's most local, or regional, or national. Then later we walk out on the wharf with lots of other people and watch the ferry come in from the Magdalens. We don't know anyone, we just like being there with people, the arrivals and departures, the lights on the water.

Connor seems to slip some days. His left hip gives out and he'll miss a step. Those days he presses closer to me as we walk, and my hand goes to his hips, my touch like a rein, to help him find his way. Other days he runs ahead, the sun and breeze feathering his black coat, the planes and reflections changing, like light on the waves.

I never have to say, Connor, take care of me. Watch over me. We do it for each other. When he was young, he was a talker, a crooner. I could croon out my sadness, or my joy, and we'd echo each other until my laughter won the day. He can't sing like that anymore: his old dog throat can't make that music. But he can still lie with me, watch over me on long journeys when I need to rest alone. Or annoy me with whining or howling and his incessant push to explore, to establish quick territory.

I know he won't go easy. My heroes won't.

They'll rally and rage, stumble, go down hard and take my heart and insist on getting up again. My mother and my dog, tough heroes to take or leave. A hip gone, some guts removed, doesn't matter, they'll bite back the tears or howl out their discontent, breathe hard, then rise again for the next fish to catch or roll in.

I showed Mum the place near Margaree where Farley Mowat's Boat Who Wouldn't Float is, and we went to Mabou where the different Rankin families live – Mabou and Mabou Mines. It was Sunday and we'd missed a big ceilidh the night before – one of those things that happens when you travel. We'd decided to stay put a few days in Cheticamp, where we felt like we could be at home in our cabin, and Mum could rest.

At the museum in Mabou – An Drochaid (The Bridge) – they keep genealogical and historical records. It's a centre for music and poetry and Gaelic classes. A few tired partied-out people greet us, say, You really missed something, and I'm sort of sorry but not sorry, too, because if we'd kept running harder and harder to get to every-thing, we'd have had nothing. So we go way back to the water, down to the wharf, take our thermos of coffee and some meat pastries we've had in the fridge a day or so. It's one of those tired out Sunday mornings, where there's a hint of fog, and you're out there alone, knowing everyone else is home by the fire, drinking tea or reliving the night before.

I never finished telling you what happened with Donna, Mum says, throwing some crumbs and meat to the waiting gulls.

I tried reasoning with the doctor, she says. There was my daughter, in this operating room, her dead baby inside her. I won't forget the cold metal, the echoes and overhead lights. Donna looked up at me – I won't forget that look either – and said, Mom? Why is the doctor doing this to me?

I told her I didn't know. But I think I did. At least, I was getting pretty angry by then.

Mum's standing looking at the water, and I throw scraps to the gulls.

Mum said she went to Donna, took her hand, said: I don't know why they're doing this, honey. I don't bloody well know.

She tilts her head down a moment, pinches and massages the bridge of her nose, breathes deeply.

Yes, I do know. I know bloody well.

They're doing this because they're bastards. They're doing this to punish you for not doing it their way. And they'll only get away with it over my dead body.

I was so damn mad and I felt so bad for her.

So that's when I walked over to those big double doors to the hallway.

I've thought of my mother alone with my sister in that room. I've pictured her sorrow and rage. I've pictured it and pictured it so often now that in the doorway, I can see someone standing. She's a large woman. She moves behind my mother, who is straightening her spine. The large woman squares her shoulders, and my mother squares her shoulders. My mother begins to move forward, and Edna Mae Grady moves with her. Those bastards, my mother vows, can't get away with this.

You know how you spell out swear words letter-by-letter? Like S-H-I-T? Our mother stood in the doorway of that operating room, and when no one would listen to reason or even pleading, she started spelling it out for them, very loudly, into the hospital corridor.

I said, You better get an O-B-G-Y-N in here pretty G-D quick. And they did.

I can listen to my mother like the prairie, the shifts of colour and cloud, the power of flood and tornado, the exhaustion of silt and ruin, the picking up and starting again. I can listen to her like a river that strikes down buildings, that exhausts itself, once ice floes have barged and crashed and wakened us in the night, a river that leaves behind warm pockets of silty water, for corn to grow and children to run barefoot.

I am alone in Halifax. I go to the museum, near all the construction by CBC and the hospital grounds. Huge marine animals, great whale bones and carvings, are suspended from the ceilings, as if swimming above me. And then there is one small display that I have to look down at, as if at a child's homemade and earnest display of playdough figures at a natural science show. But these figures are so perfect that I gasp and burst into tears. For God's sake what is wrong with me? I think, and just keep on weeping. I am looking at two woolly mammoths and their baby, stark cold and huddled, pawing in the snow near the frozen shores of the Bras d'Or.

Each small compartment in my mother's van is full of stones. Each stone is from a Cape Breton beach or the rugged shoreline of Freeport.

One stone is the perfect image of a child's foot, as if the foot itself left an imprint, deep, that filled in with rock and became solid over the years, and the older softer part washed away. It is like holding a child's foot, like a bronzed shoe, in your palm.

It's the right size for Maggie, my mother says.

Maggie, my niece, my mother's granddaughter, is six years old. Maggie can plunge her bare arms into a vat full of suckers and leeches to choose the best one for fishing. She can watch them cling to her arms then peel them off.

This footprint came from a child like Maggie hundreds of years ago, my mother decides as she climbs out of the rocks. The child stood here by the ocean, and she began to climb as the tides rose, like we're doing, and her foot caught in the rocks.

How did the imprint get made, I ask, like a reporter trying to jab holes in her story, or to make the jello of it firm up.

It was clay, the rocks had clay in them, and her foot became caught in the crevice, and night was coming, and the tides.

Then how did the imprint stay if the tides came? How did she get out, Mum?

Shhh. This is a story. For Maggie. Listen.

We stop to catch our breath, and in the silence, there is wind, there is the sweet smell of bayberry and juniper over the salt and seaweed, there are bird cries.

My mother sits on the shelf of a rock, and I sit by her. She begins:

The little girl, hundreds of years ago, with blonde hair and a small strong body, called to the gulls and the birds, to the haglins and the crows and the ravens, and they carried her.

My mother looks to me.

I will accept this.

She continues:

Do you know across the ocean you had a grandmother on your father's side who lived in a place like this? A great great great great grandmother. Grace Darling. Yes, that was her name. She may have been an aunt. That, too, is all right. Yes, she was real. She lived by the ocean. This ocean, in Scotland. She rescued shipwrecked sailors, on rocks like these.

I accept this, too, and think how Maggie can draw a sad dark picture in pencil, then cross it out, and next to it paint the same scene happy in water colours and sunshine. She can stand in a trance listening to the inside of her head.

So can I.

Your grandmother or your aunt – it doesn't matter – heard the screams and moans of those she hurried to rescue, sailors and fishing people whose boats smashed on rocks like these. Her long skirts and hair were drenched in salt water. Her hands gripped the pointed rocks, and like your feet, hers scrambled and clung and felt the way, the stretch and hesitation, the faith the earth and her body would hold her.

In my ancestor's body I see Maggie's, small, sturdy and strong. I see my own. Her long blonde hair falls in bangs and curls. She can gaze in the mirror for an hour, brushing and rebrushing her hair.

Strong like Maggie, like you, my mother says, maybe her hair blonde, too. Maybe days she brushed it long and wavy, maybe days she pulled it back into a ponytail and plunged her hands into the fish bait, forearms sluiced in scales, a woman of the sea and cliffs.

Maybe she left her footprint on cliffs on her side of the ocean, and over the years her footprint filled with sand and hard clay in the sun and wind and water, and today she gave it to me, so I could give it to you.

BONE MARROW

Somewhere in Michigan I buy bowls of hot take-out soup. Why we don't stop to eat at the restaurant I don't know, but we're on the way home, and logic doesn't always prevail. Back on the road Mum says, Let's stop somewhere by the water.

I see a pullout to water. I hit the brakes. Soup flies all over. Mum starts laughing. I start crying. For God's sake, get a grip.

We're exhausted. The night is dark, rainy and windswept, the roads narrow, the headlights blinding, and we are only 50 miles from my parents' home after driving thousands of kilometres these last days.

My mother has said, We'll take it easy, but she is so close she can smell home. She wants no more late night

motel rooms found on the outskirts of Sudbury, or northern Quebec, not even beautiful lakeshores and corridors of
maple. She wants her own dog, and her own veranda, and
her own husband, and her own newspaper and grandchil-
dren, and her 50th anniversary just days away.

But we, experienced travellers, are at the point of
hallucination when a heavy Minnesota rain begins. What
would seem normal in daylight on dry roads, becomes
panicked windshields where the blades can't scrape fast
enough, horns blare and distort like high school demon-
strations of the Doppler effect, and I'm whimpering, I
can't see, I can't see, I can't, and begin to pull over where
there is no shoulder. My mother, not knowing, thinks I
have completely lost my power to sustain, her daughter
has finally cracked, and right there, reduced to tears, is a
child again. She reaches to steady the wheel.

No, Mum, I say, I've got it. Somehow I have glimpsed
a turn-off in the dark, and a lit building along a side road.

Connor has been crying throughout this horrid
stretch of road, his arthritic bones tired from three days of
travel. He stumbles from the van, and we simply stand
there in the rain, trembling from tiredness and cold and
from what almost happened.

Connor doesn't head for the bush, but straight for the
garage where light glows from two open bay doors.

We just see light in the rainy, dark, sick with anxiety,
night, and the dog, I expect, is about to pee on something,

or knock something over in his frantic need to run.

Oh Christ, I say, and race after him, grabbing my Nova Scotia rain gear, the scent of bleach and fish blood blossoming again in the damp night air.

I see a man across the shop on the phone; he is alone, and there are new cars, Ferraris, Porsches, sleek, long and low, reds and silvers, all around us. He signals he'll only be a minute, as if I'm a customer come for my car. I stand for a moment by a round white picnic table just inside the bay doors. It's a strange place for a table, stuck there as if bidding us to enter.

I grab Connor's collar, drag him out to the bush, where he finally pees, then walks calmly with me to the car and my mother.

We agree to go ask the man for directions. We introduce ourselves, ask how far the road is in this condition, and when to look for the exit.

His name is Joe Elias. He asks how far we've come. 700 miles today, I say. Thousands in the last few days, says Mum.

You should rest a while, he says. Please stay and have coffee with me. It's almost time for me to leave and I've just made a full pot.

My mother and I look at each other. We've met enough strangers to know there is no threat in his offer, only the kind of invitation strangers make when they can see more clearly for a while than we can. He smiles when he learns my mother lives just a few blocks from where his father used to run the family grocery.

With the coffee and his presence, and just by stopping awhile in the light and calm, we can begin to recover, regroup, pick the metaphorical gravel from our bloody kneecaps.

Together, my mother and I, we begin the story of our travels, the ocean and the music, tacky wax museums and the dizzying ride at the amusement park, the thousands of miles of rolling highway.

We exaggerate our stories, bicker and laugh over details for this first audience, and I suspect he understands and enjoys our performance, as if he wants our company as much as we need his. He tells us what Minnesota lakes he likes to fish in, and my mother knows some of them. I ask if he'd like some smoked fish, and walk out to the van to fetch him a bag of Bay of Fundy cod smoked in a backyard in Freeport.

Outside, in the fresh air, the rain has stopped. My breath is strong and sure again and I do a little minuet, finger on top of my head as I pirouette in a puddle.

When I come back inside, he takes the fish to a small kitchen. When he comes back to our table, he sits down quietly. He puts his hand on Connor's head, strokes him, and the dog leans into him. And he strokes him again.

I wanted you to stay, he says, until you're ready.

He pets Connor again.

Then he tells his story:

My son was driving home to Minnesota from Kentucky. He was 40 miles from home. He should have stopped to rest, but he was too close to home. He hit a bridge and was killed. He was just 20 years old.

That's why I want you to stay with me until you're ready to drive again.

Mum and I didn't know what to say right then, except thank you, and really mean it.

But I can't help be struck by how little there is to say in a story like this. How short his story is. Maybe it is so fresh it is still hard to tell, or even to say his son's name.

I think of him often, and wonder how many times he may have to try it out before he can add much more to the story. And then later, I think of all the stories, and how sometimes it has taken generations before they can be told and rounded and passed on.

Then he asks, Do you have a camera? And we do, of course. Let's get some pictures of your mother in the Ferrari, he says to me, and so Mum crawls into the low-slung red car, and we really ham it up. She tosses her scarf out the window like she's Isadora Duncan and waves her hand side to side like the queen. I hitch up my pantlegs, revealing a bit of skin like the old come-hither hitchhiker pin-ups from the 1950s, except I don't have a billowing dress, just the raingear, and the big black dog, who I'm restraining from peeing on the car tires.

We got lots of good pictures, and later I sent him one.

Back at my parents' house, I ask my mum to look at family pictures with me again, because this is my time to concentrate, get it right, fill in the gaps. Try to stay inside the journey like you always do for the first few hours when you get home, before regular life robs your concentration, your otherness.

I also ask my dad about his stories, and he promises to tape some of them for me. Stories about working out on the Hudson Bay, about his family. He had a little brother who died, too, but he can't remember his name, just the white coffin in the living room.

Right now he sits across the room with their dog, Casey, on his lap. Connor's on the rug, and Mum and I look at photographs. These ones are older, go further back than our baby pictures.

One picture in the album is of wolves on the tundra chasing a moose. I describe it aloud to Dad over in his chair, and he's pretty sure he took that photo. Three wolves, the lead wolf with its head thrown back and baying, as the moose stumbles through crusted snow and vine maple.

In a small snapshot, Mum poses with her friend, Mona, at Niagara Falls. In another they perch on huge boulders in Petit Codiac, New Brunswick, a cock-eared dog by their side.

There's a photo of Mum's French boyfriend from St. Boniface – before she met Dad – striding the winter prairie with backpack and rifle and snowshoes. He is an outdoorsman and artist.

Another is of my mother's French teacher, from grade school. He sent her postcards when he travelled. He made the piano hum when he was home. Next to his picture, in white ink on the soft black pages of the album is written, Honi soit qui mal y pense.

My mother says that means All that glitters is not gold. Others say it means Shame on those who think badly of him.

That's the one who molested the boys, Dad says from across the room.

She says, Yes. I know. And turns the page.

Later she tells me that teacher was tender to her, saw her best, her dreams, her talent. Believed in her and told her so in an era when "stupid" was the word used to describe women. Stupid woman, she had heard so often coming from the mouths of others. In any anecdote about a woman, the limpet-like adjective was "stupid."

Many years after the photos were taken, her teacher was charged with molesting boys in those class- es, and she'd never known.

As she tells me this, I wonder how you can explain

that you are sickened, yet there was something there that was missing in other men.

He was not just gruffness, coldness, brush-aside toughness. He was that rare person saying you are valuable, you have things to say and be and you'll be good at whatever you choose to do.

I could see that, could see it in the picture, a man telling my mother you have something to say, you are smart and talented.

That's why it's not so hard to understand many years later, when my father told her the teacher was charged with molesting boys, how she got so mad at my father for shattering her faith. Of course she knew it was the teacher she should be mad at, that he had fooled everyone, including her.

I think in me it would then have shattered most everything, any faith he'd helped me build in myself. I'd probably crumple, conclude the belief in me must also have been a lie, the encouragement and praise must have been a lie. For a long time anyway.

But not my mother. She does not deny what the man did. But she will not, never did, never will, discard the belief he gave her in herself.

A friend asks me, How could she grow up so strong if she heard stupid so often? Nana heard it, too, I said. And so did I and all my friends. Didn't we grow up with Stupid woman driver? Stupid bitch. Stupid cow. Stupid cunt. Stupid, stupid, stupid, stupid. Didn't we take strength from wherever we could get it?

I want her geography in my bones, but her politics are the white cells in our marrow. The names CCF, Co-operative Commonwealth Federation; DFL, Democratic Farmer Labour; NDP, New Democratic Party; League of Women Voters; the Winnipeg Labour Hall, Tommy Douglas and Stanley Knowles; small meetings of women and men, in her childhood and our childhood living rooms.

Honey, you're no damn good unless you're on somebody's shit list, she says to us when we're in trouble. Mothering words to sustain us, unusual sustenance, I know.

There is something about the shin bruises, about our battle scars and laughter, haunches blue from the skid on icy grasses. Field hockey players, our legs like young strong horses, the stop start turn of the barrel racer, the yip-yip-yip of a coyote or the wolf's howl, shrieking banshees. All our battle gear in the prairie sun snow wind, the staunch way we lean into our sticks, eyes long to the far end of the field, or short to the attack, flat-sided, rounded sticks ready, hips strong and swivelling, yelling insults and imprecations, swirling in the dust or slimey just-thawed grass from the first freezes, girl-women laughing and exhausted, panting, preparing for the next onslaught, feeling the muscles and voices and crawl-if-you-have-to and get-up-again that will take us through life.

The picture album is snapshots from the 50s, the kind with serrated edges, eight shots developed and bound in a tiny cardboard file.

The baby in the picture sits in a mud puddle in her splattered white t-shirt, smiling, muddy pudgy palm raised high in a moment of joy, mud, sun, and water. It's like that picture of my mother with the same kind of sheer joy of living on her face. She's 74 years old, on a Nova Scotia lobster boat, the Bay of Fundy behind her, her right hand held high waving her hat, her left hand high with her fish, a moment of glory, sun, and water.

In that first picture, the one with the baby that is me, there's another figure, one you don't see. A woman stands behind my mother. The woman calls her a bad mother. Because it is 1953, and polio could be in that water where I sit and make mud pies. This is a terrifying time. Polio could be anywhere, could take your child and cripple her. Do not let her go outside. And if she does, in a bonnet, bound in a stroller. Careful to avoid others.

It's like a Red scare. Terror and watchful people and avoidance.

But my mother does not succumb. Instead, she uses common sense, doesn't send her children deliberately into danger, but lets us play near the river flats and gardens, where the pheasant and deer come, down by the old cars our neighbour uses for parts, in fresh rain water, in mud puddles in the sun. And tells the scolding voice behind her that her children will play in the mud and please go away.

Today I picked up two girls hitchhiking. They were beautiful and young, buxom and slender. They'd come west through the mountain passes yesterday. Hitchhiking like we did years ago. For years my girlfriend and I hitchhiked as a team, moving through small towns, or long cold prairie nights, meeting truck drivers, hearing and making stories to last through thousands of miles and as many cups of coffee and Husky burgers. Some people told us we should be terrified, and some moments we were – when the risk we took tested our skills and our communion.

I look at the two girls I have picked up. They've come three days from California, up into Alberta, through the Crowsnest and west. They take care of each other, watch out for each other, they tell me. Good for you, I say.

We won't live our lives in terror, they say.
We won't be confined to the home.

There is one other photo I always look for. Me, bare chest-
ed child in swimming trunks, four years old, standing next
to the canvas wading pool our father built. By my side, far
larger than me, is our retriever, Dinty. He is always with
us. He is fierce enough to kill river rats, shake them to
death and lay them at the doorstep. Gentle enough to
bring birds to us, to set them at our feet, then watch them
fly away.

The family photo album ended when I was a teenager.
Other albums picked up later. For a while we all went our
ways and no one put them together.

There aren't any pictures of when Mum left.

It's funny how other stories can be so full of colour,
how I can imagine Nana's needlepoint, or the train's
shriek, but this part of my own story seems flat still. My
main memory of that time is not the smell of the cookies
baking, but baking them and seeing them eaten. The
memories are more of running hard each day, miles, at the
edge of the prairie, miles and miles to exhaustion after
playing field hockey for hours before.

We lived in Manitoba, in Brandon. My mother

hadn't wanted to go back there, but went with my father for what was going to be one year. And then it was two. Then three. And when it was four she knew she had to leave. Maybe, like Edna Mae Grady, she had to say, To hell with this town. But this time the person she had to save was herself.

I hear her voice like the river, see her hair in the breeze as she sits on the old log, with the gardens and Red River behind her, and I run to her on chubby girl legs, and I will run that run forever, and her arms will always be stretched out to me.

I wasn't young anymore. I was 17, my father and older brothers working, my older sister living away on her own, my younger sister still home.

By then my mother had read *The Feminine Mystique,* and she'd read *The Stepford Wives.* The confined and safe rebellions of the *I Hate to Cook Book* could no longer contain her.

I don't think this is something she would ever have seen herself doing, leaving the family. And the day she left the house haunts her still.

I can't recall the specific time she talked to me before she left us, maybe a lot of times. I was old enough and enough of her daughter to understand. I know now she'd seen her mother have to make a similar decision, to walk out, and eventually, as in her mother's family, my own family came back together.

Just as her mother had trusted her, to use her instincts

and common sense, just as my mother trusted me to do the same, I in turn trusted my mother.

And in that year, I ironed the clothes and made the cookies, for my brothers and sister and father. I ran miles each day after school, bashed and screamed and slid my way across the hockey fields, read late into every night, began writing for keeps, and kept hoping Mum would find what she needed, and come home to us. And she did.

I think in that time I began to understand about being a woman and a mother, and trying to write at the same time. Those years, both when she was with us and when she left, are so mixed in with the voices of my teachers. The rich mixture of Welsh and Irish, Ukrainian, English and Scots, reading us stories aloud, urging us to write.

I've looked in my trunk over and over, amongst the old school term papers and small newspapers I produced. I'm looking for the poetry I wrote then. I can remember writing about her in the way we were assigned to write in the metre of Dylan Thomas, long strung out sentences ripe with adjectives. I remember writing to the wind even then, and if I close my eyes and fold my hands in prayer, the words written in my teenage hand do come back to me

...*race you homeless winds across this prairie ocean, slip through my window's yawn, then screaming moaning to be released, I'll trap you in this land of peanut butter sandwiches and security...*

and then I can't remember the rest except the wind got

free and left me there alone in my room. I think I let it go. I think I opened the window. I think I said, Run, Mum. Run.

I hope I did.

Somewhere in that time, I can see in hindsight, I began to know I couldn't manage school and writing and mothering and friends and boyfriends and eventually working for a living. Some people can, but I can't. And maybe then I decided that each part needed your guts and soul. I understand now that a story when it's growing can't be put aside, no more than a child can be. Some stories need to lie fallow a while, to have their own time to mature, untouched. But a story in birth, just born, can't be walked away from. Or it will be cold when you come back from the things you think more important. It will have grown colicky or resentful. It may have died. It demands as much belief in its birth, and its right to be, as a child does. When faith falters, so too does the child, or the story. I am building faith and stories, and I am drawing strength from somewhere. Some way of surviving, some understanding of grandmothers and great grandmothers and mothers and prairies and solitude, and the hard choice they each had to make, even once in their lives. I think now that I have made that hard choice too. Not to marry when I had the chance, not to leave these mountains that compress me, not to leave my nights alone. I know life will change, and the sirens will sing different songs. I hope through it all to be as strong as the narrative links I am forging.

I know my mother might have been a writer. I know in her circumstances it wasn't possible. I know she wanted each and every one of us, even though she had to leave us for a while. She waited until we were old enough, and then she did what she had to do to preserve her sanity. Maybe I said that to her, like she said it to her own mother.

If I didn't say it before, I say it to her now.

We are all together, family and extended family, for my parents' 50th anniversary. My parents look shy and proud as they cut the cake. All five of us kids make short speeches. We don't think of Donna, the youngest, as the speech maker, but hers is the most thoughtful, the best.

The anniversary is over, and on my last day in Minnesota, Mum is driving me to the lake, where we'll say goodbye, and Connor and I will climb back into my own old car and head home for Canada.

We're out on the secondary highway, like many of the roads we've travelled on our way to Cape Breton and back. We're alone again, too, so it's a satisfying moment of taking up our trip just for a few more miles, taking care of that empty ache you feel when a long journey's over.

Mum's looking straight ahead at the road. She's been quiet for some time now.

The other night, she says. At the garage.

Yes, I say.

What was the man's name?

Joe. Joe Elias.

When he told us about his son, something happened that I couldn't tell you right then, because I thought you'd had enough for one night.

What happened? I ask.

You wouldn't have seen it, she says. You were sitting directly across from Joe, absorbed in what he was saying. I was looking past him. And as he began talking, a shroud of mist moved into the doorway. I know the night had cleared, but it was there. It lingered there, as if it were the son, and in the father's telling, and our listening, was witness to his own re-creation.

ASSINIBOINE WRITING

strain to catch CBC again as I head north by a different route, through Bemidji, which I can't even recognize anymore, back into Canada. It's past Labour Day, and I don't realize that places I wanted to see – Louis Riel's House and the Living Prairie Museum in Winnipeg – have closed for the season. Winnipeg is so familiar to me. Though I've never lived here, we came here often when I was a kid, to see uncles and aunts and grandparents, and later I came here alone as a teenager. The roads make sense, even with endless construction. Moir's Osborne Drugs was on Osborne Street near the Golden Boy on the Legislature. The Bay where Mum worked was on Portage. The boy I had a crush on lived off North Main. My two sets of grandparents lived on Sherburn and Toronto Streets. My brother Brian lives here still.

I have a sense of direction here which I can never find in Vancouver. I am at home here, steady.

The Living Prairie Museum is closed, but they've told me I can take the self-guiding trail through the 32 acres of tall grass prairie and 10 acres of aspen preserved in the city. The area seems familiar, then I realize I'm near Nana's old nursing home. I try to close my eyes and ears to the joggers on the track nearby, the modern brick apartment buildings, the Friday afternoon traffic on Ness Avenue, the airplanes.

I am wandering through the kind of prairie my nana and mother once walked through. The walking tour shows me how delicate is the old prairie, how hard to bring back once invaded or disturbed. It guides me to golden rod and silverleaf psoralea, and the big bluestem grasses that have turned red and will soon be the colour of straw. The brochure tells me bluestem was called turkey foot because of the three toes of the seed head. Standing in the rain which is beginning to chill this fall day, I spread the red toes in my fingers and they look exactly like a turkey foot.

I am learning more about the prairie I grew up in. I even find out what tumbleweeds look like before they dry out and tumble. I wallow in a buffalo wallow, a depression grown in with grass, as big and deep as a buffalo. In my brown leather jacket, I'm a small buffalo, my back on the ground, rolling and scratching, my eyes on the sky.

I shake myself off, walk through all the acres, and finally into the small deserted grove where there once was a homestead. In the clearing the house would have stood. And though the flowers are gone now, you can see the lilac and caragana bushes. It is so quiet in here, and cold, and I am alone. I am glad I have a coat today, and pull it tighter around me.

I wish Nana could be with me here. To walk in this place with me. I would put my coat around her, put my arms around her. I wish I could give her that comfort, instead of the only one she could find the day William died.

I try to imagine what every Valentine's Day after that, Valentine's and all its chocolate, must have been like for her. I wish she could have smiled somewhere down the line, after telling the story too many times, maybe even adding some bravado, how she marched around that block, cold as death itself, ate some chocolate and then faced life square on. She could say only chocolate could revive her that St. Valentine's Day. And then I think maybe the wind was too strong, or the pride or the guilt. On the prairies, the less said the better. Least said, soonest mended.

Then later I figure out, this is how I cope with loss, too. Alone at first. In the cold if I can find it. And then I'll tell one person.

Then even later I think, Nana did tell her story to one person, the right person, my mother, and now I have heard both their voices, telling it to me.

It's getting colder, and I suppose I should be frightened, alone here hidden by bushes. I'm not afraid, because in some way I'm not alone, and it seems okay to move on, now that I've understood something, and given something back.

I re-enter the open prairie. At the big buffalo rubbing stones, where the buffalo rubbed the boulders shiny, I plant my spine against them and give myself a scratch and a rub. I'm alone and laughing.

I walk along the Assiniboine, remembering my high school writing project about it. Backtracking and eddies, an intestine of a river, the sternwheelers stuck on sandbars, crew and passengers hopping out on the banks to collect firewood and lighten the load as it fights its way around another curlicue – and the passengers trip through the woods to meet the riverboat and reboard around the bend.

I realize now that this is my pattern of writing and thinking as well. A convoluted Assiniboine way of figuring things out. With backtracking and eddies, getting stuck on sandbars, a lightening of the load, and the reboarding, refreshed and ready.

I say goodbye to my brother Brian, who hugs me and helps Connor into the car, and we leave Winnipeg, head to La Rivière where my mother was born. I know there's a woman there who knew my mother as a child. For a while I don't know if I'll take the time. The relief of yesterday's rain is over, and again it is so hot, and so far to home and the trip has been so long already.

Before I left BC thousands of kilometres ago, I had had my brakes redone, and I had experienced no problems since. Nearing the area where my mother lived, I think I've picked up a rock in the wheel well. I am inclined to fast driving so I won't hear it, but some nagging voice urges me to slow down and pay attention. The mechanic at the garage in Manitou says the wheel is about to fall off. How could I not smile to be in a town with the name of Manitou, spirit, the name Manitoba comes from, and be saved from an ugly accident, simply by listening to a voice whispering in my head? One of those moments when you say, all right then, what else should I slow down and pay attention to?

After this, I decide to take the time to look for the woman who knows my mother. All I have is a recent picture, but no name. I've lived in small towns enough to aim straight for the credit union or co-op store for this kind of intelligence. At the La Rivière Credit Union, I explain my mission, and an employee tells me the woman's name and helps me call her.

Ethel Davidson is 83 years old. She's had three heart attacks in the last year. She invites me for a quick lunch, as she's rushing back to Manitou to play piano for seniors in the hospital. After sandwiches and coffee, she draws me directions on how to find my mother's old place, more detailed than the map my mother gave me, pats her old retriever, Tessa, on the head, and asks me to come back in four hours if I still want to visit.

I don't want to be left here alone right now. I want and need more of this place I have just heard so much about from my mother.

I can't say, Please don't leave me. And I'm not sure how else to behave. As a reporter I'd have grabbed my crutch, the tape recorder or the job, and used it as permission to insinuate myself anywhere. But this is her first performance in a long time, she clearly wants to be alone, and I am no longer a reporter. As she drives away, I stand alone in her yard.

I don't know of anything to occupy four hours, and it is staggeringly hot. I take a picture of La Rivière's giant wild turkey near Kim's Lucky Dollar General Store. I walk up the store steps, go to push open the door, only to learn that it is closed for the lunch hour.

I walk along the road, looking for the CPR station where Gramp worked. But it's gone. I feel strangely homeless. I feel like my mother when we first got to Comber, so many expectations, and instead standing there so empty and shrunken.

I decide to head home to BC I pull Ethel's small map from my pocket. I'll take another stab at this searching, I guess, and take a drive past my mother's old hillside on my way up a dirt backroad, Route 242, the Somerset Road.

On the long road there, I stop, uncertain whose directions are right – my mother's or Ethel Davidson's. Ethel says it's just after you drive through a really deep gulley, but our concepts of deep gulleys, hers Manitoban, and mine after 20 years in BC, are different. I am confused, caught between definitions, and I realize how long I've been gone. Then I try to see it with my mother's eyes, the ravine she called that "godforsaken hillside" in all her stories, and I imagine it in winter, with wind and blizzard. I stop, take pictures of prairie and ravine and drive away, heading for BC, not knowing for certain my mother had ever stepped foot on that patch of ground.

I feel ambiguous, empty.

I drive for two hours, arguing with myself, the voices all my own.

Fool, I think. What's wrong with you? You should have stayed to talk to her. Go back.

No, that's stupid. It's a waste to drive all that way back again. You should have thought of this before. What if she was only being polite and didn't mean it?

Finally, I veer off the road, get out, stomp around and curse all my voices. Now they're arguing over the nature of what's more frugal, going on or turning back. The third part of me can't believe I am having this debate with myself on a dirt pulloff.

I spin around and speed back, as if a flashy exit has at least the dignity of a decision. As I return to La Rivière, I see thousands of blue dragonflies above the yellow canola and blue flax. I meet a man taking his Percherons to a parade, and he invites me to come see them tomorrow. I chart a different route and swoop into more of the spectacular Pembina River Valley. I've heard the word Pembina roll off my father's tongue a hundred times, talking about botany trips there. But I haven't been here since I was old enough to walk. At the meeting of land and sky, on the crests of the hills, huge rolls of hay stand on edge looking down at me, the monoliths of this prairie Stonehenge. Buffalo look up at me from the shade of trees in their ravine near the water.

Two hours later Ethel Davidson looks surprised to see me. She is exhausted from her afternoon. Oh God no, I think, I've made a mistake after all. When she offers Connor and me a place in her home for the night, I am sickened to think I've encroached too far on prairie hospitality. Instead, I book into her son's motel, at the La Rivière ski hill, and take a shower while she rests and watches *The Young and the Restless* on TV.

Later, I go back to her house, right on the banks of the Pembina River. She invites me out for supper, and we talk about dogs and politics and jam recipes and stem borers in the canola and single women running boarding houses and how her mother ran the hotel, about political campaigns and the little she remembers of my mother. She tells me she would never live without a dog. She tells me she bought Nellie McClung's house and had it moved here, to save it from some fate, and now it's part of a museum back near Manitou. At some point this visit moves past being about my mother, and becomes this woman and me having our own talk. About life in La Rivière, the life in Winnipeg, about coming home to a place you left long ago. She invites me back to her home, and shows me pictures of her journeys around the world. In the evening more strangers arrive at the door – friends of her son's she hasn't seen for 30 years. I take a picture of them all standing together by the river. Later, I ask if she's tired. I want to know if I should leave now. Oh no, she says, I'm not ready for bed. You never know who might knock at the door next.

That night I dream about a wolf. One of its eyes is blue. It appears hungry and seems to be threatening me. I call a man who has a gun. Then I look more closely and understand the wolf is trying to take my hand to guide me somewhere.

In a second dream, a man I know is trying to molest me. I am running from him. We are on an island. I grab my clothes and purse and canoe paddle and run. I am terrified. My dog is waiting for me on the other shore. I cross the river and reach him. Weird, I think, and wonder where that dream came from. I think of my old dog, Connor, and Ethel's old dog, Tessa. I'd never live without a dog, she'd said.

When I leave Ethel this time, there is more peace in me. I am more familiar now with these lonely backroads, able to travel them alone, to stop and leave the car behind and walk amongst them.

The wind sweeps the grasses in a soft way today, small gusts that make me laugh. I look over at Mum's ravine where Nana and the wild women played cards. There are no more of Nana's wild women on this hillside. There is not even a shack. Just a ravine, and wind, and a long look across the prairie. Like the buffalo jump, somehow.

Long ago my mother's brothers, now all dead, came out from Winnipeg and burned the old log house, a dangerous eyesore.

There is really nothing here to reconstruct it, only wind, and scraps of stories.

I could simply ask my mother for details, but as I stand here, I want to make my own, see with my own eyes. I want to listen, let my mind go in the little shimmers of heat rising from the earth, those shivery moments when the wind stops.

It doesn't even matter any more if I'm not exactly in the right place, because somehow I am. It's even okay if

I'm on a different hillside, if the pieces and times become confused, because I'll slide them back together in my own Assiniboine way.

Maybe if I tread softly, I'll be allowed in. If I close my eyes long enough, listen hard enough until I hear their voices on the wind.

Some barrel staves lie rotting and shot through with sod. Are these what she skied on? The five miles uphill to school and five miles uphill back, that we always heard about when we complained about our own walk to school?

The logs are soft prairie alder and spruce. Strips of cambium still hang from some. The logs are dark and mildewed from the holes in the roof. At home in BC, my own logs, harder woods from the Interior forest, larch and fir and pine, mildewed too as we built and lived with makeshift roofing.

The pump would have been at the kitchen sink like the beetworkers' shack where I lived in southern Alberta. The table is a drop leaf – I still have one – and pressed back chairs.

I wonder what Nana cooked. I'd like to stand near enough to see the set of her jaw, the soft down on her cheeks, as she pours oats into the large pot of water. I'd like to help her put food on the table, while watching my mother tussle with her Airedale puppy underfoot.

My mother is wearing a dress made out of a flour bag. I'm thinking for a moment of potato bags – coarse gunny sacks, from all the potatoes they must have eaten – and I wonder if many froze, went mushy sweet and black, like in the potato famine. But that's letting myself slip too far. I can see Nana's stitching in the little flour sack dress my mother is wearing, a small piece of colour and beauty in this starkness.

Cats run in and out the window. Standing here, alone, in the wind, all I can think of is badly chinked logs, and screeching cats tearing through, cold water and screaming snow, and where, my God, are any neighbours? And Gramp is away in the big strike.

Nana is staying here, trying to maintain it all, still wondering how in God's name she got here. Maybe she stares at the glass in the window long enough that she sees William, but she knows he's not there, and she turns back. She shuts her eyes and presses her hands to the edge of the counter.

The wind gusts through the house, empties my ghosts. The chandelier for kerosene lights hangs above the table. It's the one they played cards under. There are no lamps left, and the cord is frayed. Perhaps she took the lamps with her.

There's only left what she didn't take. The little scraps you forget or abandon when you finally close the door and run, slam the car door and don't look back.

On the dusty counter, there are dry mouse droppings and a dead sparrow, and a small leather bag, a tobacco bag, chewed at and frayed. I'm surprised the mice left anything.

I touch the bag with my fingertips, and roll it gently into my palm. It is as light and skeletal as the sparrow. But it can't be mistaken. My mother called the opening a "star twist." It took me so long to understand what she meant. I twisted it, she said. I was a baby and I kept gnawing on it, and twisting the opening, open and closed.

Were you so hungry? I asked her. No, we were hungry then, yes, but I chewed on it because I was a baby and I chewed on things.

If I twisted it now it would disintegrate.

A poplar tree, probably just one more whip sprouting along the house when Nana took the kids away from here, rubs against the roof, scraping and sighing like a horse scratching its shoulders.

Nana finally pushes her hands from the edge of the counter, turns and notices what her one-year-old is sucking on. She grabs it from the baby, upset that in her reverie, she has been negligent again. Of course she's seen tobacco bags before, but not here, not this. She twists it open, and looks into the dark opening.

Nana puts her hand right here to catch herself. Then with sure but shaking hands, she removes five dollars from the tobacco bag.

She looks to her daughter, then runs for the door and calls the boys. Boys! She shouts and calls them by name.

Boys, you can go to town now! You can go to town.

Five dollars! We have five dollars! Her voice would be

firm and strong, almost crazed, and she would swoop my mother from the floor, and the boys, aged seven, eight and nine, would head for town, remembering the chant she made them, their simple grocery list:

The mail

The cream can

The paper and the bread

And she would add to the list, like any of us who ever get bushed living in a cabin too long. She'd run after them, she'd name the bright colours of cloth, she'd name sweet things, like licorice and chocolate. Then she'd pick up my mother and swing her around and around.

I turn west at an intersection north of La Rivière, stop and watch the crop duster swing low next to me, in the last attempt to save the canola.

I won't head up to the #1 just yet. I'll stay on the backroads a lot. I'm leaving my mother's and Nana's territory now, pushing further west into my own parts of the country where they have never lived, meeting people they've never met.

It's months since I first stopped at the Captain's Table in Weyburn, but I'm glad to see the same waitress. I wriggle past the vacuum cleaner stashed next to the table back by the restaurant kitchen. The waitress has just slipped in a quick round of vacuuming, sucking up the morning's toast crumbs, before the lunch rush. I haul out my decrepit scotch-taped maps, not because I need them to find the way anymore but because they show where I've been, and because they're as familiar as my old dog.

I settle in and listen to the kitchen chat, the orders coming and going. The waitress is calling her kids at home before the lunch rush begins, saying Hi, remember not to call during lunch now, then comes to my table. I order a fishburger. Maybe it brings a smile, some recollection of my fisherman friend's preference for haddock over cod, but there's no pang in this. It's just a fishburger, that's all. The waitress adds a generous shake of chips to my plate, a nod to a travelling sister, a waitress of the spirit, as if we all can tell who's been one, and who has never thought sitting near the waitresses is an insult. Then coming over from the dessert counter, she selects for me the biggest piece of carrot cake, with the thickest icing I can eat all the way to Maple Creek, licking icing from my fingers as the tornado warnings come over the radio and the buffalo crowd in their corrals.

I would like to live at the Maynard Motel on Main Street in Moose Jaw. At least it is a place I know I can feel at home, pulling into the driveway, like into our old red ranchhouse on the Red River, rippled glass brick windows in tiny squares. They know I'm the woman who drives across the country with the big old dog. We have our routine (avoid the nasty alley dog who flies along his run chain, hurling his body the allowed two feet into the back lane before the line to his throat yanks him off his feet).

In the Maynard Motel there is a desk big enough to use and Connor knows the backroads.

At the Husky in Medicine Hat, across from the Ranchmen, back where the old woman blessed me over the Cream of Mushroom soup, the silver circle spins with my order fluttering under a black bobber, and the waitress sets out coffee for the regular before he's in the door.

I point out to her on the Husky place-mat map how far I've come today, and we talk about travelling and weather and storms, and exchange the I-went-to-there, and I-came-from-there stories, between pouring ice waters and coffees, and she opens up my take-out bag, and throws in extra packets of salt for the margarita I've told her I'll treat myself to tonight, and she reaches for the chocolate give-aways and throws some more of them in, too, and says, Hey, good trip. Drive safely.

I stand outside my old shack near Lethbridge, on the road to Diamond City and Picture Butte. Sometimes I'm afraid to stop here, because I'm not ready for it to be gone, not ready to stand here and imagine it.

It is full of my own stories, so real in every shovelful of dirt we dug, that it takes me months before I can see how like my Nana's shack it is.

The windows are boarded up. Poplars that were saplings 20 years ago tower and bend, their thin and tentative voices now a full choir. I stand and listen. At my feet, the foxtail swish and dance in the lower decibels. In this house we pumped water at the kitchen sink. Dirt and snow made small drifts inside the windows, and cattle scratched their shoulders on the siding's asphalt shingles. From the prairie here I could look west and see Chief Mountain in the Rockies a hundred miles away. I could watch as two lines of clouds met, opposites colliding, stretching to the horizon, deciding the weather. This house is where my sister came after she lost her first baby, and in this house she lay while her baby cried to her each night on the wind. I'm not sure I know the words the wind is singing to me now, so many years later. I only know the harmonies are as familiar to me as if they are my church, and I have finally returned. The wind surrounds me, soothes, cools, enters my lungs and plays in them as if they are caves made for echoes. The wind is hot and demanding, it sucks and lifts and throws its voice. It is a moan and a summons, the depths of its deceptions and layers of trust as complex as the ocean has ever offered. I nod to the wind, bow to it, kneel to pluck some foxgrass, which I carry home through the Crowsnest, and keep in a blue glass bottle until its seed heads have blown across the floor of my cabin in the bush.

ENGAGING THE HEAD

Homecomings are difficult. I am restless and edgy, not ready to be here. Over the years friends have learned to leave me alone a few days when I return. Though my valley is beautiful, my home well cared for in my absence, I feel hemmed in, anxious, sick with words.

The mountains hold me down and sit on me. They clamp my shoulders, wire my jaw.

I turn off the phones, the radio, put signs on the door saying Stay Out. I am hounded by dreams and strange sleeping.

The mountains press me until I resist, scream at their darkness, tell stories to defy the darkness.

I rise late and sleep early. I wake in the night. There are voices in me and they won't stay quiet. I can't shut them out. I am sick without them. Sleeping and waking, I strain to hear the flute entering amidst the fiddles.

The mountains squeeze me to explosion, like fire on the cone of a yellow pine.

I stand at my kitchen sink, staring and listening to the prairies as the foxgrass sways and spreads itself open, and those moaning winds won't leave me in peace.

Their voices won't settle until I've said them with words, until I can understand their language, as if I am a visitor to their country, exhausted with the struggle to understand, and they will not leave me to sleep until I do.

Listen wind, listen buffalo; I am trying.

The wind is the sound of their babies' voices, a grandmother's and later a granddaughter's. Both moved to shacks on the prairies after these deaths, maybe the only place they could walk alone, allow themselves for a while to hear voices, where the prairie itself was the symphony of their mourning, the train whistle, the going and gone, the comfort of knowing it will come back from another direction, another place. A wolf's howl deep in the coulee, when you put your head down at night, wondering how you could cry so long, and the wolf raises its throat for you, does your crying for you to let you rest. The shush and sweep of the grasses, a brisk shove of wind to keep going: scurry, coat-bound, for the chores or work in town, or gentle, gentle, shush, sweep. Rest and sleep, rest and sleep.

Did my sister conjure her baby? Did my Nana conjure hers?

Could we all conjure each other for a while?

Could I?

Could I conjure, too? Could I call my mother, could I conjure my dog, for the while it takes, until sometimes it will be years before I need them?

My mother will come to me each time I need a smart remark, when I need to square my shoulders in a doorway and say, To hell with this town.

My dog, as my old cat does, will he appear to me in my dreams when I am in deep, deep trouble?

My mother can conjure, I know. Not by tricks or will. But by her willingness not to wear her skin too tightly, that others who've been shut out too long can come share her warmth, share their stories, know their voices will be alive again in her retelling, her re-creation.

Am I conjuring her now, at the Buffalo Jump, in my dreams, am I making her separate while calling her closer, taking the clay of her and moulding it my own way?

Shaggy in our big prairie coats, big furs, we bunch our shoulders, like the buffalo, charge the wind, eyes half-blinded squinted shut in snow. Our big coats let us keep going, leaning into wind, not like those who never know cold, who don't understand grim, and the hot rush of blood in the warmth later. Those of us who can run hot and cold and take it, keep some neutral place

inside our buffalo coats, some silent place while heading to bed down on the prairie.

I'm trying ways to figure this out, this stuff about where I
belong, where I can live. It seems wrong to live so long
here where I feel like a stranger, not to the community, but
to the formations of earth. To want so often to leave, then
finally come skittering back to brood and fret.

My life here in the mountains is a combative debate
with nature. Mountains stop me, they are too convoluted
to cross, too dark to enter, too snowbound to exit at will. I
understand two things: that these are ungracious emotions
for a guest of 20 years, and that somehow I belong here, at
least for a long time.

I remember first moving here, seeing fallen grain
sprouting in a friend's dirt-floored garage. Oh, it's so easy
and lush compared to southern Alberta, I thought. It's so
easy when nature is not trying to beat you. But there are
different kinds of beatings – too harsh a word I know. But
in Alberta where the wind can freeze you, it can also cool
you in summer, wrap you round and sing to you. The sky
opens its stories to you, storm fronts colliding and dancing for you, northern lights romancing you.

I'm beginning to wonder if transience is as much a
heritage as is rootedness. Maybe roaming large territory,
calling many places home, is home for me. A neighbour in

Nova Scotia once said my family's roots are wherever we put them down. I took it to mean a welcome to settle and stay there. Now I see it another way, that I may have many homes. That my roots are mycelia.

Dreams that started two years ago increase – of buffalo, babies, wolves, deer, my mother, wind. Some of it is images and words. Some of these dreams seem so obvious now, but at the time they only fled past me at daylight, or stupefied or tripped me in the busyness of the day. Sometimes I'd wake up crying, or just roll over and bury my head in my dog's shoulder.

I begin to pin up my pictures from the buffalo jump, of dark tornado skies, of my old prairie shack in southern Alberta.

I start reading more about the prairies. I see that my family's movement is like an old prairie habit – Manitoba, the Dakotas, Minnesota, across to Ontario and back, and out to BC In the movement, our stories got scattered like milkweed on the prairie wind. Or simply packed away in boxes that never were re-opened.

I reread my high school newspaper project, remember doing the research for it in the morgue of the *Brandon Sun,* reading issues of the *Brandon Mail* from the 1860s and 1870s – stories of Riel, of dread diseases and wondrous cures, agricultural implements and temperance songs. I read pioneer's diaries, and stories of the buffalo, archaeology and histories, biographies and short stories. I learn things I've always known, I learn new things. I begin writing down facts about buffalo.

The buffalo jump, perhaps the wind there, comes to symbolize all I care about. I can't explain it. Some of my friends can only imagine blood and gore. I know it isn't true, that for thousands of years that jump meant survival, feasting, stories, transitions. And somehow, it is forcing me to find my own stories and create my own transitions.

I ask my mother if she's heard of the buffalo jump. I am sure she'll know, that an image, a place and belief so powerful is one where we'll share some communion, as we had by the gravestones at Ingonish, or on the rocks of the Atlantic. But she doesn't know about buffalo jumps. And the buffalo were gone when Nana moved to the prairies.

Yet I've always known about them. I've lived in parts of the prairies my mother and grandmothers never lived. I've known the word piskan, or piskān, buffalo jump, a Blackfoot word meaning "deep blood kettle," as if it were part of everyday speech.

For me, the buffalo jump is no more about slaughter than is the contemplation, imagination and peace that I feel in a cemetery. I know it is a place that pushes me to take a long view, to find the horizon, to listen deeply to voices inside and out, a place that offers me peace and strength when I am alone. And I begin to understand this is the place I will return to, when I have to find my way through the biggest loss that will ever come to me.

I now understand that on this trip I have seen buffalo only when I stopped speeding, when I travelled back, actually stopped the car and said to myself: Go back, you didn't pay attention and you are a fool. I would turn around and go back to a small town on a prairie backroad, to see a church or a small museum, or to go visit someone who'd said, Stop by. And then, later, as if in reward, I would see the buffalo. If I squinted my eyes, I could blur the fenceline that contained them.

One hot August afternoon I had driven while listening to tornado warnings, in a trough of weather in southern Saskatchewan, the kind of weather as kids we'd run shrieking through before being herded into the basement. And there, again, huddled against the coming weather, were the buffalo. Face front to the challenge. Shoulders strong. Stance quiet.

It wasn't a conscious decision, like I'll take a backroad and go slow and see the buffalo. I realize now that it only happened if I made a good decision, when I yarded myself up and redid something, if I took a risk and said, Oh no, I have to do this. I won't get this chance again.

A friend loans me an old journal of an explorer on the Hudson Bay. I read diaries of those with a lust for wandering. I wonder who fits this definition, if it can only be men in the cold with teams of dogs, or if I can redefine it to include the women I know who prefer the backroads and finding their own homes.

How can a woman be both the adventurer and the core? The centre holding, yet also the wanderer?

Refreshing herself, recreating herself as a stranger amongst others who expect nothing of her but her outsider's eye, relishing their centre, their core.

Her celebration of them in turn becomes their celebration, and she carries home with her a bit of their strength to feed her own.

A core needs a wanderer, and a wanderer a core, to feed each other, like fresh air, oxygen to enrich the blood, mint to stimulate the lips, nettle to sting your fingers, snuff for the sinus, red pepper for the gut, long prairie for the eyes, rich clothing for the skin, textures removing you from t-shirts and the same backyard garden.

Sometimes she comes home too soon, continues to fret, not having learned enough, not having yanked her potbound roots enough, not scruffed them up, broken some, wriggled the others loose enough to let them grow in new directions, in soil she has excavated so thoroughly that when she returns, she can put her feet down, splay her toes and they will not feel pinched.

When that happens, she can become core again, sturdy stem growing and flourishing, offering, drinking in, until some shoots fail, roots overwatered rot, hit clay or snarl around themselves, rootbound, and need wrenching free again.

I think that writing, like a woman, can't be confined to the home, or it will consume itself. It needs space to wander, be scoured by wind, lie on its back by a river or in the stubble below a prairie sky, to fight blizzards and icy roads.

I think all the words have to pass these tests. If they remain confined, they may become crippled like bound feet, like ulcers, like suicide.

The animals become more insistent. They seem to bang on my door and say, Hurry, hurry, before you can't come with us anymore, can't hear the voices anymore. As if someday I could no longer believe, or the spoor would all be gone, and I could no longer follow. Come now, they say, taking my hand, or walking through my walls, into my dreams, within the periphery of my vision.

Don't abandon your old dog or your old car, they seem to be saying. You need some strange edge of howling and rust so you can be on the borderline, where this contact is possible. In a new car, new clothes, air conditioning, new dog, the windows won't be open any more. Your old dog won't wake you whimpering in the night. Right now, you must not go over, break faith. Later you can, later will be okay, but stay with us now. Stay in the woods with us, making your firewood. Stay in the wind with us, hearing the voices. Stay alone at night, even if the horoscope says you will fall in love on Sunday after dark. Soon. Not yet.

I dream I am approached by an incredibly handsome and naked young blonde man, with a wonderful twinkle in his eye and a hard cock. Can I just kiss you? he says. And there is a playful and promising peck. No, young man, I can't do this, can't even do it a little bit, I say resolutely. I know I'm too much like Ado Annie. For me it's all or nothing.

Can I crawl in and hold you? asks my tempter. I could learn to be family, says this waif. He crawls in a moment, not touching, and then the old dogs, Connor and his friend Sadie, guardians of my chastity, my celibacy, begin barking in the dream, wake me up, and I say, "Begone, young man," and he vanishes. And doesn't return.

I become busy again. Political campaigns, press releases, working for a living, making check marks next to chores accomplished. The wolf dream recurs. This time there are several wolves, and they are starving. I am at the edge of a town, and rifles are pointed at the animals running toward me. I look more closely, and push the rifles away. The wolves are dogs. They are trying to tell me something. They are begging me to pay attention.

EYES ON THE HORIZON

can still drive my old car, the odometre this time at 290,000 as I set out one year later. But this time Connor will stay home with a friend.

His black hair is shaved from the crown of his head down to his shoulder blades. The skin is grey, the flesh swollen and hard. Tubes drain eight puncture wounds. A week ago when he came home from his daily rounds, I think, Oh, he's rolled in the mud, the hair on his neck wet and thick. But when he leans against me, and I bury my hand in his coat to give it a good ruffling, my fingers come away thick with blood. He's been savaged by another dog, a visitor to the neighbourhood, staying where Connor goes each day to say hello to a female dog friend.

I go to speak to the dog's owner, a young man. He sits on a large rock, rolling a cigarette, an act that can speak of friendship, or of an arrogance buying time and distance. Your dog looks all right to me, he says. I look at my beautiful old Connor, who now is so frightened he won't leave the house without me, not even to take a pee. I look back to the young man, and have rarely felt such fury. He could say, I'm sorry for this mess. We could each give and take over the whole thing and finally understand that both our dogs are responsible. But he simply tells me my dog is old, his dog is young, and that his dog won.

I want to take this vacuous young shit, beat his head against a tree, press the life from him. He and his dog are bullies.

Instead, I yell at him, say useless things like, Now listen here, young man. Insist that his dog be tied up and walked only on a leash in the time they stay here. It is small satisfaction.

The drive now would be too hard on Connor, the prairie too hot for him to breathe. I have never travelled without him. I take him to my neighbour's early so he can't see me pack my bags.

Right through the Crowsnest, I catch myself turning around to talk to him.

At the Maynard Motel this time, the woman asks me where my dog is. I avoid the corner with the nasty alley dog leaping at its chain.

In Winnipeg, a historical society gives me a lead on how to find the Nellie McClung house that Ethel Davidson told me about. There are two such houses, both at the Archibald Farm Museum on a back road between La Rivière and Manitou.

On the phone to the farm museum I say that Ethel Davidson told me about the house last year and I'd like to come that way again, see it and visit her.

Ethel died yesterday, the farmer tells me, in a voice that is matter-of-fact, but not unkind.

She died yesterday? I repeat, as I look across the room to my brother.

Yes, he says. Her funeral's on Monday.

My brother, Brian, starts looking through the papers for an obituary, as if to put an anchor on this news, to find some way to make it more normal.

I set down the phone, and repeat the information that she'd had three heart attacks, dealing out facts to take away the strangeness of the moment. I tell him again how she played cards with our uncles, and knew Mum as a little girl, and how she welcomed me.

And yet I know damn well that I almost blew that visit. Almost drove away. And that repeatedly that day, I couldn't help but feel some grace, some intervention, that something had taken my hand and helped me forward, and when I resisted, gave me a good tug.

Today I wear my new sagebrush-coloured sweater, clean blue jeans, and black hook-up boots, not the usual sloppy summer clothes. I want to be prepared for this museum, as if for church, some structure and lift in me. Some respect for the places I enter.

At the museum, down the backroad, a man and woman are watching for me, an off-season visitor. They welcome me, invite me into their home. They show me the La Rivière anniversary book, *Turning Leaves*, and I point out my uncle's pumpkin-faced school boy smile in a class photo my mother had shown me.

My $4 half-hour tour lasts two hours. I am walking in some kind of daze. Here is the old CPR station my grandfather worked from, the one I couldn't find last year. It has been moved here and is being restored. Here is where my mother ran in and out as a child, the station Gramp came home to when he was sick with the flu 78 years ago. Here in Nellie McClung's home is the clean cool smell of old prairie houses. Here are yellowed newspaper clippings taped to the walls, detailing the politics of their times. Here are things you can touch and hold, not partitioned off or behind glass. The man lets me touch velvet quilts in the log cabin pattern, woolen long johns and handmade lace. We look at the buttonhook boots, and I lift my foot to show him the ones I am wearing. A daybed in the kitchen is like those I've seen in Nova Scotia; coral flowering geraniums in the bay window are the same as those in my own home. There are few possessions of Nellie McClung's; there are no icons on pedestals – This Is The Teacup She Drank From in 1911 – no, instead on the walls are handwritten quotes on yellow pasteboard, her descriptions of these rooms she loved, and the people here have restored them by the light and texture of her emotions. Here are sets of her books, and that's what matters, and the man here has read them. The neighbours have contributed their finest petit point and children's nightdresses, their books and chiffonniers – it is their collective record of the times and the community. The houses transported here have stood here now so long they belong, surrounded by pink mallow, like roses, and lilacs. I think of my nana and mother, living so roughly on a hillside just miles away, and I wish they could have known this. I think they would have been happy living in these houses. I could be. I could sit down right now at the table by the bay window, set Nellie McClung's notebooks to one side, and bring in my own from the car. I could gaze out the bay window, smell the smell of this old house, walk the creaking floor, love the light playing on the walls. This place lets me talk about my mother and grandmother. This place lets me talk about Edna Mae Grady, about Gramp and the 1918 flu.

Sometimes I simply stand and hold my breath, thinking of the work, the love, represented here. I don't usually use religious words, but I feel somehow blessed because I was told about this place, because of all that went into bringing me here. The photograph my parents gave me of Ethel Davidson, the wheel ready to fall off my car in Manitou, the argument with myself on a pullout, the dream of the wolf taking my hand, old dogs and dreams and grandmothers, and the buffalo again and again.

On the way down from the second floor, I stop to let my eyes adjust in the dimly lit staircase.

Before me hangs a buffalo coat.

I touch the coat, put my cheek against it. In another museum I would never presume to touch, or ask. But today, here, I could believe that I am allowed, even supposed to ask. Could I put it on? He smiles at me, and removes it from the hanger. I carry it to part of the room where I won't knock over her books or tumble over the pressed back chairs.

The coat is stiff and long. Maybe the man helps me into it. Maybe not. I only remember stepping into it. I am inside it. It covers me completely. I reach behind me in buffalo hide arms and raise the collar, bunch my shoulders. The man is watching from a respectful distance and is smiling. I am watching from a respectful distance, too, watching in the mirror a woman in a buffalo coat. And I am smiling, too. It's as if all the animals in my dreams, and all the women are smiling at me, too. You have paid attention, you have come through a hard time, you are growing up. You can curl up with us in here for a moment. We give you this moment to take you through life.

I guess I just stood there for a few moments, then realized my left hand was shoved into something in the pocket. What's this? I ask, barely able to withdraw the object or move in this large coat. He helps me, and we pull out an empty mothball tin and a packet of coloured chiclets. He doesn't throw them away. He returns them to the pocket and places the coat back in the recesses of the stairwell.

Bob Wallcraft, the farmer-curator, asks me if I'll join him and his wife, Darlene Henderson, for lunch. For the first time on this journey I feel complete peace and belonging, as if all the pieces fit. Standing in this prairie farmyard, near my mother's birthplace, with a man who has read and restored, this man and woman who care about the same things I care about, that my mother cares about.

At the kitchen table, we put together tomato sandwiches, with pears and coffee and homemade cookies. In this Manitoba kitchen, as in rural Nova Scotia kitchens, the scanner chatters and blats and now and then we stop our own talk to listen. Bob's sons are talking with their wives, keeping a line open from distant fields where they work, keeping in contact just like the fishing fleet did from the Bay of Fundy, for safety, for the sound of other voices, and the exchange of mundane domestic detail.

Out in the car, I have some cucumbers that my brother sent with me. Are you sick of cucumbers? I ask. I've been sick of them all my life, Bob says, so I give them to Darlene.

As I head west I pass a dappled fawn killed on the highway. I think of the buffalo coat. There is a howling in me, and I pull the coat tighter.

By the time I reach Weyburn, my hair's blown all around from the turned down window I call my air conditioning, and my face is brown and freckled. There are bug guts smeared like egg yolk all over my windshield. As I pull up next to a police car, the officer looks at me and the rusted-out car, and when I ask where's a motel, he hesitates, grins and asks, An inexpensive one?

The next morning I see an "Elk Crossing" sign, and it jostles into position the dream last night of the elk and buffalo storming a back corner of our old beet workers' shack west of Lethbridge. They gouge and rip with their antlers and horns, tearing off asphalt shingle siding, already weathered and ready to fall. We beat the animals back with baseball bats, swinging the bats around our heads like lariats, kiyi-ing and shrieking and running at them before they knock holes in walls that have so far held against wind and cattle. Finally the elk and the buffalo turn away their great heads, their massive shoulders and hooves, and thunder back to open prairie. They appear to be laughing. I am laughing, too. As if it's a game we've been playing, and we all know I've been fighting them as hard as they've been bugging me.

They know and I know this message is not about an issue, furs or meat or saving the seals. They know I've butchered bears and chickens, and though I haven't for years, I could and would do it again. It's something beyond that. It's something they'll only tell me if I go enough places alone, small motels on the edges of prairie, where I'm alone, sleep alone. They won't come to me if I am buffered by another human. They'll come to me if my dog and cat are near. I am beginning to learn their language, and I can sense their patience, though sometimes they will jostle each other, as people will do at a joke, and I think their amusement is in watching me, their puppy. I'll live past any one of them, but their young ones, then their young ones, will wait for me.

I drive through the far southern route of Saskatchewan

and Alberta, south of the Cypress Hills, on a lonely Sunday afternoon. I am tired and have forgotten it is Sunday. Gas stations are closed, the roads almost deserted, the weather shifting from hot to stormy, and the road heavy going with newly laid gravel. I put the car in four-wheel drive, as if pushing through slush. I feel the need for human voices, many of them, in harmony. I turn off the quarrelsome whining voices on the radio, reach for the tapes with lots of people singing together. I reach for music from Cape Breton, fiddles and piano and voices, and they lift me through the last long stretches of gravel. The weather shifts rapidly from overpowering heat to stiff cold wind and rain. By the time I reach Fort Macleod the weather is nasty, and I am thankful for my lined leather jacket, and for the bright and warm colours in my room at the Fort Motel. Above the bed are matching nautical wheel lamps with orange lampshades. There are orange towels, and some orange table tops. There is plenty of room to walk and stretch, to set things out, notebooks and take-out food, make-up kit and suitcases. I take a walking tour of the town, peer into stores and the old theatre, feel safe among human voices.

In the morning, the rain smells of mown fields. I wake early, make my thermos of coffee, select the same clothes I wore to Nellie McClung's house, stop at the bakery on the way out of town, get a great big fresh and sticky apple fritter.

I'm going back to the buffalo jump. The roads are almost empty, it's raining, the car heater blasts perfectly, my fingers are sticky with icing, and the coffee is fresh and strong.

Maybe I can be alone out there again at the jump for a few moments.

This time I spend more time below the cliffs, looking closely now at the bushes and grasses. Shirley Bruised Head from the interpretive centre first lends me a plant book, then comes outside with me, and maybe my father's years as a botanist, the years we heard the Latin names, the prairie grasses, the summers at biological stations, are beginning to take hold of me now. I find myself sketching prairie grasses so I can know their names, rough fescue for buffalo forage, and needle and speargrass that would embed in shaggy coats or long skirts. The chokecherries and buckbrush, which is also called wolfberry, are so tall here I first mistook them for alder. I look for the turkey foot, big bluestem, but I'm too far west on the prairie. I do see goldenrod and sage. I look down at my new shirt, and realize why I wanted it. It is the colour of sage and of lichen on the big rocks over the jump.

I'm alone, and like a schoolchild at an intersection, I approach with caution. This is an intersection where life and death changed hands.

Stop, right where you are, below the jump or above, before the jump or after.

Look, for the wind they push before them.

Listen, to the silence later, when the charge is over, when the earth has stopped moving to their thunder, when they have finished their shifting, their shapes now the thickets of buckbrush.

Shifting like the trains and the sweep of grass across the prairies, like wagon trails rutted so deeply you can still see them trenched in the ripening grasses, like women seeking their place in this geography, pushing and stopping, reversal, withdrawal, the wind that crazes, clears away, scours, keens, pushes and sweeps like a woman cleaning the floor with lengths of stiffened grasses, broom, bluestem, bristling in the wind. Women and buffalo, moving heavy or swift, eyes on the horizon, it is the push, a wind, a going over, straight ahead.

I can't say here and now that I stood there and heard a voice or voices. Not something I could say, Oh yes, my Nana came to me, a buffalo spoke. But I heard them in the way voices come to you when you're washing dishes, looking out the window, drifting, in the way things kind of swirl together, when your hands are working and your mind is free, and the voices talk inside your head. If you are truly looking for faith, they said, this is where you'll find it. If you're not ready, you'll rush by, afraid, or in distracting company. Here is where you'll see the bones you need for your structure, here is the wind for your lift. Not just our bones, but the strength of them that you need for your own.

The bones and stories will be your spine, the strength your toboggan, the coat will surround you, the wind will give you comfort or command.

I understand now that there are places on the backroads that leave room for dreaming. Museums where every fact is not laminated, recorded on speaking headsets, the facts so tight you cannot wedge in your own image. There are places that encourage your own stories alongside theirs, places that don't give all the answers, where your own touch and walks in the wind are encouraged. Where you may find some time alone, take your own self-guided tour, where silence is the gift given. I make a list of these places, on the prairies and in the Maritimes, and the gifts they have offered to me.

The wind will give them voice. Some days it will soothe and warm, sometimes challenge, other days it will hold nothing of them. The wind will be my church. The buffalo will be my church. Sometimes I will enter looking for something, and none will speak to me. They will hold themselves apart until I have prepared myself. They will not speak or show themselves, the motels will be mediocre, museum attendants will be bored like robots, if I am not ready, if I am too full of myself. If I have not emptied myself, prepared myself alone. They will raise their barriers. I will be one tourist too many and they'll have no stories to tell but what is paid for.

Like me back home in BC, they prefer guests in winter, when they've been alone too long, and stories are ready now to be told.

MAKING MY WAY BACK HOME

I say Ptui to the auto wrecker who offered me $150 for my car last month before I left the mountains. Ptui, I spit out the window as I pass his shop on my way back from the prairies. I speet on you! I yell again out loud in some kind of spaghetti western Italian mama mia imitation. Ptui! This $150 wreck and me just put on 5,479 kilometres for $199 gas. The doors may not lock all round, but there's nothing to steal. It's gone 120 km/hr illegally along with everyone else, except uphill. As easy as slicing pie it's shifted into 4WD in the deep gravel of southern prairie backroads, when the wind and gravel swung us along like a boat.

Back home, I collect Connor. The tubes are gone, the hair coming back. He's still afraid to go on his neighbourhood rounds, but now his friends come to him. One morning I look out my window to see my 13-year-old dog engaged in a salacious romp with his old girlfriend, the one he got beat up over. I am laughing so hard that I call the vet to report the progress.

I gather what I have of my Nana's, like a child making her treasure trove of feathers and rocks at the ocean. I have her recipe for oat squares, written in my mother's hand. I take from the wall her needlepoint, the colours of roses and violet in the walnut frame she made for it. I gather the homemade lace tablecloth that she made, and on top of its brown folds lay her old brooch of green rhinestone. From my trunk, I take the only two letters from her that I kept, the sheets of foolscap still folded into small envelopes. Finally, I wrap around me her Persian lamb coat.

That is all I have of her that I can touch and hold, the last physical links.

I take the recipe down to the kitchen. I dig out the oats from the cupboard, pour boiling water over the shortening. Mix in sugar and flour and soda, then open my front door, step barefoot onto the chilly brick porch, leave the batter outside in the night to harden.

She is always in a cooking apron, pheasant bosomed. She is always wearing a coat and hat. There are always children in the house, neighbours, uncles singing at the piano. There is always a veranda full of plants. There are pug-faced bulldogs underfoot.

I remember the smells of face powder and pound

cake, as we swung along Portage, bags in hand, after our excursion to The Bay. I remember heavy stockings, the suck of air through false teeth. I remember white hair and coke bottle eye glasses.

I remember driving with my mother to Nana's nursing home. I remember how she became old and fragile and the rough fabric of an armchair could rip her skin, so paper thin it could hardly be stitched back together.

And years after that I remember standing with my mother at the funeral chapel in Winnipeg. There was a large orange bird of paradise plant. It seemed so out of place there in the winter. I remember my mother taking my hand. I remember understanding she still needed her mother then. I remember her leaning down to kiss her mother goodbye. I remember the eulogy, and within it the stories my mother herself had written of her mother.

In the morning, I rise early, take Connor for a walk in the crisp fall air, bring my notebooks and pencil downstairs away from the computer. My Nana cannot be remembered best at a computer. Instead, I clear the kitchen table. I dig at the hardened batter, which by now looks like something you'd hang out for the birds. I press it thin on the cookie sheet, as my mother's writing in the recipe tells me to do. I'm using my hands, push, push, and I see Nana's hands strong again, the skin firm.

Score the batter, it says.

I score it, place it in my old gas oven at 375°. The

electricity goes out, but the smell of sweet baking oats fills the room.

In my dreams for years now the animals have kept coming.

They are pushing in, trying to tell me something as they barge around and take my hand. Even in their intrusion they don't scare me. They are dancing, pivoting on sharp hooves, barrelling around with their shoulders, raising small tornadoes in the dust.

It's trite, perhaps, or presumptuous, to think there's something out there helping me. But I don't have God or Mary or Jesus. I never rejected them, they were just gone from my family before I was born, except as figures in someone else's literature.

But I guess I had to conjure something to help me through the hard times. At least she has her faith, I've heard it said of people who pulled through, overcame.

And what faith is mine, beyond some fierce belief that people are good, that tomorrow will be better? What images of strength are there bigger than my own repeated beliefs, which some days can be kicked and shattered like rocks cracked with fault lines? I look at the wall before me. These are the pictures over the last few years, since leaving Nova Scotia. Coulees, the Atlantic, long grasses, the buffalo jump, buffalo and wolves, snow drifts outside our old prairie shack, gravestones of miners in the Crowsnest, full of stories. There are only two pictures of people: standing by oxen or buffalo. I look at these pictures and know they are my bones and sinew, my rock and my lift.

It's okay, Nana. It's okay, Mum. It's okay, buffalo and wolves. Your stories will be in me. Sometimes I will wear your coats. And sometimes you will sing to me. And sometimes we'll all go separate ways, or we'll be silent. But I have to thank you. I have to say this grace to you, for coming to me when I was alone.

The buffalo hunt was blessed before setting out on the prairie. The fleets are blessed before setting out to sea.

What movement of a woman ever was blessed before she set out?

God bless Nana for the moments after her
   baby died
God bless Edna Mae Grady for her largeness
   filling a door frame
God bless my mother for jumping for the train
God bless great grandma Alison for leaving a
   drunken husband and setting off on her
   own for Winnipeg
God bless Donna for hearing her baby's cry on
   the wind and making more babies
God bless a great great great great for her sturdy
   body trusting the rocks and sea
God bless their Scottish spines that straightened

and endured
God bless their Irish souls that made stories to
make it all bearable

From this place, this distance, this wind, I can finally hear them. In this quietness, I can begin to hear their voices, as they themselves have heard voices in the wind.

A prayer to all women, that is what my Buffalo Jump is. Huge imagery for what often is lost, or never even told. I want a prayer to them, a monument as big as cliffs, as strong as wind, as silent as alder.

I want the small walk Nana took to be a mile in silence. Mother's jump to the train a mile in laughter. The voice of my sister's baby a train whistle shaking the prairie night.

I want the broken stories to be told.

These small movements, the taking in of air, the leap, eyes on the horizon, they are our buffalo jumps, our movements that shape our lives forever.

In my home in the mountains, I have just been to a meeting of our local burial and cemetery society. We've learned to handle the practical matters surrounding death and burial.

It's the night of the lunar eclipse, and occasionally during the meeting someone jumps up and runs outside to check the moon. But finally we are too engrossed in details, bogged down in by-laws and in the size and shape of headstones, and forget the moon, until a girl sticks her head in and says, It's happening! We rush out, papers in hand, and binoculars are passed around, someone explaining that the earth is passing between moon and sun. When I drive home down the valley, I choose the open highway rather than the backroad, which is closed in by trees. I crane my neck round to see the big clear moon in the big clear sky, just a shadow of eclipse like a crescent hanging on. I consider what fun someone could have with headlines if I crashed, while moon gazing, after attending such a meeting.

I pull into the meadow by my community hall and my house. I have never seen the field so bright with frost and moonlight. In the middle, the doe and her fawns stand and graze. When I walk toward them, they look up, then let me come nearer. There is only the sound of the deer ripping up frosty grass, their hooves, their breath and mine. We cast long shadows, taller than ourselves. Tonight the mountains are friendly presences ready to protect, rather than imposing, looming, taking over. The field has never seemed so big, the mountains so pulled back, as if they have taken their bow, slipped into the wings, given the stage over to light. I stand a long time with the deer, until finally it is too cold and the eclipse is finally over. The deer step into the bush. I walk from my old car inside to my fire and my cat, Dylan, and my old friend, Connor.

That night I dream Connor comes to me, carrying something soft and white in his mouth. Dylan walks with him. They sit down before me. Dylan watches, and I realize she has been nursing this baby. Connor lies down, sets the small animal between his paws. The animal nestles for a moment into his chest. It looks to the cat and dog, then for the first time, tries its wings and flies away.

ACKNOWLEDGMENTS

To editor Bonnie Evans for the incredible hours of work and always the right questions

To Coteau editor Bob Currie for the fresh eye and fine work, and to Gwen and Bob for their hospitality

To Coteau's Nik Burton and Geoffrey Ursell and staff for professionalism and courtesy

To readers Sabbian Clover, Julian Ross, Ruth Porter, Shirley Bruised Head, and Lynne Van Luven

To Caroline Woodward and Sally Mackenzie who kept close counsel

To the Hallatts, Moirs, McLaughlins, Chris Callaghan, Steve Krambeer, and the Crockers

To the strangers who opened their doors – Ethel Davidson, Bob Wallcraft and Darlene Henderson, Eileen Curry, Joe Elias, the neighbours of the Margaret Laurence home in Neepawa, the young woman in Comber, and the waitresses along the way

To Shirley Bruised Head, writer, and education officer at Head-Smashed-In Buffalo Jump Interpretive Centre, Alberta

To the writing and reading community in the Kootenays that promotes, values, and supports working writers

To K. Linda Kivi, who set in works the notion that anyone receiving some writing money gives some to another writer

To Marcia Braundy, stalwart neighbour and friend to both Connor and me

To Paddy McGurin, for her help when I most needed it

To Marianne Hodges for the French

To Dr. Elizabeth Barbour for medical information

To Rick Dillabough, information officer for the Brandon Wheat Kings, for fact checks

To writing retreat buddies, Vi Plotnikoff and Caroline and Sabbian, and all the deer out in the backyard

To Norma Dann, who wrote a family history that intersected with my own

To the wonderful writers and songwriters and singers in this country, who write about who we are, and who make great travelling companions

To the founding members of the Dead Dog Society, Sadie Brown and Annie, and now Connor

To Connor and Dylan, and to my 1984 Tercel 4WD, which cruised through 300,000 kms and never gave up heart

Head-Smashed-In Buffalo Jump near Fort Macleod, Alberta, was designated a World Heritage Site by UNESCO, the United Nations Educational, Scientific and Cultural Organization, in 1981.

RITA MOIR's first book, *Survival Gear* (1994), was shortlisted for both the Edna Staebler Award for Creative Non-fiction and the City of Dartmouth Book Award. Her article *Leave Taking*, a true story about preparing for a body for burial, was a 1989 award winner in the *event* creative non-fiction contest, and has appeared in the *1996 Norton Anthology* and in *Best Canadian Essays*. Rita has had several radio and stage plays produced in addition to her many print and radio journalism credits.

A Canadian born abroad, in Minneapolis, Rita Moir has lived in Brandon, Lethbridge, Edmonton, Sudbury, Vancouver, Prince Rupert and Freeport, Nova Scotia, as well as in Fargo, North Dakota, and Amherst, Massachusetts. She set up her permanent base of operations in Vallican, in the Slocan Valley of the British Columbia Interior, in 1975. Rita has been a factory worker, a waitress, a treeplanter, a publicist, and a Women's Centre staff member. She is currently a guest instructor at the Kootenay School of the Arts in Nelson, British Columbia.